CHAR

C000030497

ON F
THE PEAK
DISTRICT

40 Circular Walks in
Europe's Most Popular
National Park

DAVID & CHARLES

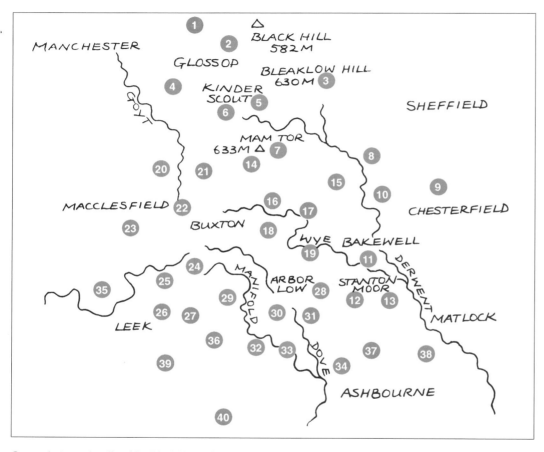

To Susie and Bruno,
my constant companions

Photographs by Mike Williams
Maps by Susannah Penrose

A DAVID & CHARLES BOOK

Text copyright © Charles Hurt 1996
Photographs copyright © Mike Williams
First published 1996

Consultant editor: Roland Smith

ISBN 0 7153 0343 0

Typeset by ABM Typographics Ltd, Hull
and printed in England by BPC Paulton Ltd
for David & Charles
Brunel House   Newton Abbot   Devon

Cover photographs: (*front*) Ladder Hill and Combs Reservoir from Whitehills (Walk 21);
(*back*) Upper House Farm in the Woodlands valley, from Gate Side Clough (Walk 5)

Page 1: Ravensdale cottages with Ravencliffe above (Walk 30)

CONTENTS

INTRODUCTION

The Peak National Park covers an area of 555 square miles (1,438sq km) and has a population of about 38,000. Most of its area is pastureland, and it includes over 80 square miles (210sq km) of 'open country' or 'access land', largely moorland, where the public is free to roam at will except for a period between August and December during the grouse-shooting season. Its only settlement large enough to be called a town is Bakewell, though many others lie on its perimeter, like Buxton, Matlock, Chapel-en-le-Frith and Ashbourne, not to mention larger built-up areas such as Macclesfield, Chesterfield, Sheffield and Greater Manchester. The Peak District as a whole extends considerably further than the Park, which stops short of some fine country on its fringes. It stretches over parts of Derbyshire, Staffordshire, Cheshire, the old county of Lancashire and what used to be the West Riding of Yorkshire.

The Peak is usually divided into two unofficial areas, the Dark Peak and the White Peak. This sometimes causes confusion. The two Ordnance Survey Outdoor Leisure maps which cover most of the two areas would be better named the North, or High, Peak and the South Peak. For in reality the White Peak – an undulating limestone plateau of high pastureland, scattered villages and beautiful river valleys – is girdled in a horseshoe shape by the far larger Dark Peak, a sombre, higher and bleaker gritstone terrain of moorland, peat hags and groughs, with strange eroded tors, abandoned boulders and cliff-like edges. The limestone country is rich in flora and fauna, with carpets of wild flowers in the spring and early summer meadows. The hags and bogs of the Dark Peak, where the mountain hare thrives, are covered by cottongrass in June and July, and there are many thousands of acres of rough grass, heather and wild bilberries.

The Peak's landscape has been created partly by its underlying rock – mainly limestone, shales and gritstone – and partly by the many changes it was subjected to over millions of years. The fact that it was once covered by a lagoon full of small sea creatures is reflected in the many fossils that can be seen on the stones in the walls of the limestone areas. Particularly distinctive are the 'Derbyshire screws', the remains of the stalks of sea lilies, creatures with five branching arms which fed on smaller organisms. More recently, the Ice Ages were responsible for the characteristic valleys, caves and underground caverns that we know today.

Early man was present in the Peak in slowly increasing numbers after the retreat of the ice, and he left behind him various remains. He was followed by Neolithic arrivals from Europe, and then by Bronze Age immigrants known as the Beaker People. The Romans were attracted by the lead, the mining of which was still the area's main industry into this century, and the Normans established the Royal Forest of the Peak for the purposes of hunting. Sheep have been reared in large numbers throughout the centuries, and they are largely responsible for the look of the pastureland today. On the moorland, the red grouse, valuable in sporting and commercial terms, has been the dominant indigenous creature for the last two hundred years. Cromford has claims to being the cradle of the Industrial Revolution, being the place where Richard Arkwright chose to build his cotton mill in 1771.

The whole is a walker's paradise. The remarkable network of over 2,000 miles of footpaths and rights of way allows almost endless combinations of routes to be devised,

The route at Oxlow Rake (Walk 14)

especially in the south. The beauty of the limestone country is in its thousands of miles of lovely drystone walls, fine farmhouses and barns, meadows of wild flowers, caves, glorious dales and sparklingly clear streams. The hills, though modest in height, are often exactingly steep, and offer the reward of superb views and fresh, invigorating air. There is a wealth of ancient sites left by early man, and the remains of an industrial past that has more recently made its mark on the landscape.

The Dark Peak rises to 2,088ft (636m) at Kinder Scout, and what it lacks in stature it more than makes up for in reputation. There are pathless tracts of wild and savage country over which conditions can be tough and exacting, where you can sink time and again up to your knees in bog and return eventually to your start exhausted, chastened and reduced. The Howden Moors, Bleaklow and Black Hill – described by Alfred Wainwright as that 'desolate and hopeless quagmire' – together form one of the last real wildernesses in England. The weather is notoriously fickle and dangerous, and can change from sunny and spring-like to awesomely terrible in a few tramps of a walker's boot. There is, however, a solitary beauty and timelessness about these remote uplands, and few places can match them in terms of challenge and satisfaction.

Parkhouse Hill (Walk 24)

Another reason for the Peak's popularity is its accessibility. Twenty-two million visits are made to the Park each year. Half England's population live within striking distance of it, while the huge conurbations that surround it account for some 17 million. This huge invasion of people and cars puts intense pressure on the countryside. Many of the more popular walking routes have suffered serious erosion, while car parks and public lavatories have sprouted over hill and dale to try and cope with the visitors' demands. I remember blissful summer days as a child, picnicking, fishing and wandering in Dovedale largely alone and undisturbed in a way that people now visiting that most popular and spoilt of dales would find incredible.

The authorities face a grave dilemma. They can continue to open up the Peak to public access by car, although no new roads are planned at present. This will mean creating more and more car parks and facilities. The snag is that more car parks means more cars. They can decide to take the pressure off one 'honeypot' area by encouraging visitors to investigate the next valley, but that next valley will soon fill up, and the honeypot will remain just as popular. Such a disastrous policy will ultimately ensure that the Peak District disappears under the sheer weight of numbers.

Alternatively they can decide that enough is enough. In my opinion this is the only sensible course. Even the Ramblers' Association – and no one has a greater belief in public access – is coming to the conclusion that it is now time to restrict access to certain areas, and to make it less easy and convenient for every car-load to drive directly to their favoured destination and admire the scenery. Yet the Derbyshire Dales District Council continues to promote tourism in the area with undiminished zeal, to the detriment not only of those who live and work here, but of those in search of the county which Daniel Defoe once described as 'a howling wilderness'. When I read that the authorities have decided to create another 'heritage centre' or signpost another old ruin I sink into despair.

There are other pressures too. The residents of the Peak have to make a living. Not all of them dislike the growing number of visitors. Many of them have shops, bed-and-breakfast establishments, pubs, hotels and other businesses which depend upon tourism. The quarries which may offend the eye of the walker or motorist bring employment to the local inhabitants. Housing or road developments may be cursed by those wishing to protect rural England but welcomed with open arms by those living in it. The work of the National Park (the first to be established in Britain, in 1951) has without doubt been a force for good. Without it the countryside would certainly have been largely ruined in the last half century, and on the whole it deals sensibly and efficiently with some complicated problems. It is not necessarily popular with the local people, however,

and not all its decisions are praiseworthy. It has made mistakes in particular with some of the buildings and architecture it has sanctioned since its creation.

Writing this book has been a labour of love. I have known the Peak all my life and care passionately about its past, present and future. My admiration for its people, especially the farmers, knows no bounds. Out in all weathers and at all hours, the sheep and dairy farmers of the Peak fight a hard battle to gain their living, meanwhile conserving the landscape we all love, and they deserve our respect.

Kinder Scout was the scene of one of the first mass trespasses in 1932. Since then there has often been a cold war between ramblers and landowners, with the former winning almost every battle. As well as being a walker, I am also the owner of land across which several rights of way run. Perhaps I am in a good position to see both sides of the fence. I am constantly reminded of the good behaviour and courtesy of the vast majority of walkers and surprised at the disagreeableness of the few. It is only the latter who seem to consider it an insult to be asked to stay on the paths rather than to roam at will, and to use the stiles rather than climb the walls. Perhaps they do not stop to consider that if everybody adopted their tactics it would become impossible to farm, and that the countryside they

The route near Alstonefield (Walk 33)

have come to enjoy would therefore cease to exist. It is they too who drop the cans and the crisp wrappers, and park their cars where they have been asked not to.

Similarly, most farmers and landowners are content to keep up their stiles and welcome or at least tolerate with good grace the often large numbers of walkers across their land. (Here, as I write, about a hundred ramblers are passing my house, some of the several thousand who will do so in a year.) It is only the hidebound and narrow-minded landowners who attempt to obstruct the rights of way and make the life of the legitimate walker difficult. Their selfishness and paranoia are increasingly ridiculous in the modern world. Visitors to the Peak will on the whole find their welcome to be very warm and friendly. The Peak District has been called the lung of England for its vital role of offering clean air, beauty and open space to those of us unlucky enough to be confined in the cities. Long may it continue to do so.

EXPLANATORY NOTE

In choosing the 40 walks in this book I have tried to avoid some of the more obvious routes. My main concern has been to space them as evenly as possible so as to show off the immense variety of scenery that is one of the area's particular joys, though I am aware that parts of the High Peak are somewhat under-represented because of a desire to avoid the over-used Pennine Way whenever possible. (For a walk on Bleaklow see the companion volume, *On Foot in the Pennines* by Roland Smith and John Cleare.)

The distance of each walk is measured in map miles, which in hill country are no accurate indication of length. To climb into and out of a steep valley might be only one mile on the map but three on foot. As an entirely fallible general rule, add on a third to the map-mile distance to calculate the true length. The estimate of the time needed to accomplish each walk is only approximately based on the pace of a reasonably fit adult. Adjust accordingly.

The maps which accompany each walk are not designed for use in the field, though it should be perfectly possible to navigate using them and the text. You are strongly advised always to take the corresponding Ordnance Survey 1:25,000 series map, as listed with each walk. A compass should also always be carried. A few of the walks require one, and others would be made easier. In certain adverse conditions a compass might be vital to your safety.

DOVE STONE MOSS

A compass will be needed for this most northerly of the 40 walks, a splendid tramp across the cloughs, groughs, peat and heather of the wide open spaces above Dovestone and Chew Reservoirs, where the going is tough, boggy and tiring. The steep climb comes near the beginning of the outing, so that the second half is downhill and easy.

Descend from Binn Green car park (1) along the Oldham Way. Turn left at the lane signposted 'Open Country' and cross the dam between Dovestone and Yeoman Hey Reservoirs. Turn right and, after a wall and before the bridge, strike left uphill, east-south-east, keeping the stream to your right. You will see Ashway Rocks ahead to the left and, standing alone to the right, the Ashway Stone. Make for that, following a fairly obvious path up the side of the hill.

Find a footpath just below Ashway Stone (2)

Looking north across the wilderness

leading to high up the brook you originally kept to your right. Turn left past a drystone grouse butt over a little stone-flagged footbridge and follow the small clough to your half-right up towards the summit. You must now head due south across the moss, where cottongrass grows in profusion in the summer. The tower on the dam of Chew Reservoir will come into view directly ahead on a clear day. Make for this. When it disappears from view, head towards the highest point of the distant hill. The moss reaches over 1,670ft (510m) in height, Dovestone Reservoir now being some 900ft (274m) below.

Cross the dam (3) and turn hard right down Chew Road beside the clough and head west-southwest turning northwest. Nimble-footed sheep will be perched precariously on the sides of the clough, and a savage outline of rocks stands out to your left like broken teeth. There is an alternative route along the Chew Brook.

At the bottom of the clough turn left and walk round the west side of Dovestone Reservoir, over the dam, and follow the path over the stile northeast along the conifer plantation, forking left back to the Binn Green car park.

FACT FILE

Map OS Outdoor Leisure 1: The Dark Peak
Start/Finish SK 018045: Binn Green car park, off the A635 northeast of Mossley and west of Holmfirth, on the right near the northern end of Dovestone Reservoir
Length 6 miles (9.5km)
Walking time 4 hours
Difficulty A steep climb is followed by a difficult and boggy route across Ashway Moss that could also present navigational difficulties. A compass is essential, and the walk should not be attempted in bad weather

The Route in Brief

1 SK 018045. Downhill from car park via Oldham Way, across dam, turn R after a wall and strike easterly uphill to Ashway Stone.
2 Path leads S from below Ashway Stone over footbridge and S across moss to tower on dam of Chew Reservoir.
3 Cross dam. Turn hard R down Chew Road beside clough, WSW, then NW, then NNW up to Dovestone Reservoir. L round it, over dam, along path NE, forking L up to car park.

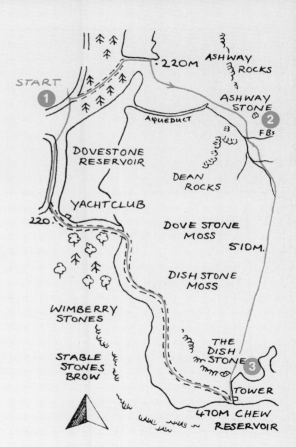

11

LAD'S LEAP AND LONGDENDALE TRAIL

This exhilarating northern walk provides a taste of the open spaces which make up much of the Dark Peak. A fairly tough climb of almost 900ft (275m) attains high moorland of solitude and desolate beauty, with wide-ranging views, and a precipitous descent leads the walker down to the string of reservoirs that water Manchester for a long tramp back along a disused railway line.

From the car park at Crowden **(1)**, leave on the path leading towards the camp site. Turn right and then left down the path over the bridge crossing Crowden Brook, and then right at the Pennine Way sign **(2)**. After a ladder stile turn left up the right-hand of two tracks, the one which makes its way through bracken west up the hillside.

Now climb fairly steeply, heading west, following the path to the left over a broken wall towards the summit. Highstone Rocks come into view a little way to the south. Cross the broken wall and follow the next one up past a small cairn, then a post, and twice across a little brook which will be dry when there has been no rain. Continue gently uphill, still westerly, following the path when the wall ends.

Now the distant rumble from the road has faded. There is just the sound of the wind and the larks. This is the Dark Peak at its best. At the top a wall begins again, but the path slants away from it towards Lad's Leap, the way marked by cairns **(3)**. Millstone Rocks are visible ahead. To the south, on a clear day, there are sensational views of Bleaklow and Kinder Scout, the highest point in the Peak. Torside and Rhodeswood Reservoirs also show themselves from the bottom of the valley, with Glossop beyond them. To the southwest are Werneth Low and Cown Edge, and to the west the eastern quarters of Manchester.

Hollins and Coombes Cloughs meet at Lad's Leap. Cross here and walk left round the rim of the hill **(4)** at over 1,600ft (490m), Coombes Clough falling away to the south. At the far edge of the clough swing down left along a path leading west-southwest over open moor drained by Black Gutter. You will reach the boundary fence of open country **(5)**. Cross Rawkins Brook and take the right-hand of two ladder stiles.

The path leads down through heather and bilberries. Extreme care must be taken. There is a very steep drop to the left, and this is not for the fainthearted. The abandoned quarry is known as Tintwistle Knarr. Skirt the plantation, cross the stile at the boundary fence and wind down the hillside to the main road **(6)**. Turn left for a few paces then right through some gates down the lane through the wood and across the dam between Valehouse and Rhodeswood Reservoirs.

Before the detestable Heath/Walker boundary changes of 1974, Longdendale was in Cheshire, part of a thin wedge that pointed northeast to Yorkshire, dividing Lancashire and Derbyshire and known as the 'Cheshire Panhandle'. This passage through the Pennines was claimed by the earls of Chester to ensure their salt could be transported east via Salters Brook Bridge (a few miles east along the A628). Now it is in Derbyshire.

It is thought by some that the Etherow River in Longdendale once acted as a boundary between the ancient tribes of the Cornovii (of Cheshire) and the Brigantes (of most of northern England, including the Peak). The dale was transformed in Victorian times by the building of the Manchester to Sheffield railway and five reservoirs which then, at six miles long, were the biggest expanse of artificially gathered water in

Looking east towards Longdendale with quarry workings above Crowden

Map OS Outdoor Leisure 1: The Dark Peak

Start/Finish SK 072993: car park at Crowden, north of Torside Reservoir on A628(T). Several bus services connect with Crowden, and Hadfield Railway Station is at the southwest tip of the Longdendale Trail from which it is possible to join the circuit of this walk

Length 7½ miles (12km)

Walking time 5 hours

Difficulty A steep climb to begin with. Paths on the moors may not be distinct and a compass should be carried. Do not attempt in bad weather. There is a descent on a narrow path with a precipitous drop on one side

The Route in Brief

1 SK 072993. Leave car park towards camp site and cross bridge over Crowden Brook.

2 R up Pennine Way. After ladder stile L up R of two tracks going through the bracken W up hillside.

3 Follow cairns at summit towards Millstone Rocks WNW ahead and cross brook at Lad's Leap.

4 L round rim of hill and, at end of clough, L (WSW) across heather.

5 Reach boundary fence, cross brook and take R of 2 ladder stiles. Descend to main road.

6 L at main road then shortly R through gates and across dam. E, becoming NE, along reservoirs for over 2½ miles (4km), joining Longdendale Trail after road.

7 When trail meets road again turn hard L down path, and cross road and reservoir. Descend steps on other side and follow path W ahead. R at fence and up to car park.

the world. They supply some 24 million gallons of water a day to the Manchester area. The railway is now dismantled, but power lines and the A628 cut a swathe through the valley. Despite everything, some sort of community spirit survives.

Turn left up the track on the south side of the dam, climb the stile and take the path ahead east along the reservoir. At the dam between Rhodeswood and Torside Reservoirs take the lane to the right and cross the road to join the disused railway line, the Longdendale Trail (part of the Trans-Pennine Trail), turning left (east) along it. After a mile and a half (2.5 km) or more the trail meets the road again.

Turn hard left down the path **(7)**, cross over the road and walk down to the footbridge which leads across the reservoir and a spectacular weir. Descend the steep steps on the other side and follow the path leading west ahead. As it diverges from the dyke, turn right at the fence and ascend to the car park.

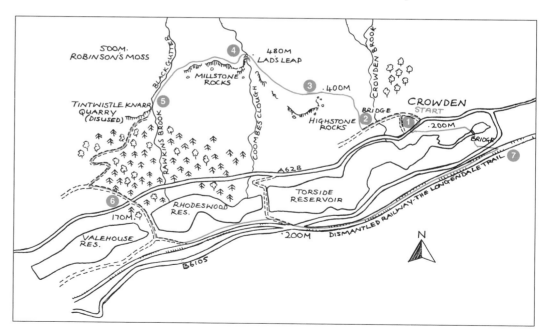

HOWDEN EDGE

As wild, remote and bleakly beautiful as anywhere in the Peak, the heather and peat bogs of Howden Moor offer the walker a wonderful challenge. A tough climb is rewarded by superb views and followed by a long and arduous tramp across the moor and along the Edge, before a descent back to the safety of the plantations lining Howden Reservoir.

Walk north through the woods **(1)**, crossing the ford, to reach Slippery Stones Bridge. This seventeenth-century packhorse bridge was re-erected here from its original location, now submerged, at Derwent and stands on the boundary between Derbyshire and Yorkshire. Walk to the right across the Fred Heardman footbridge (dedicated to a well-known walker and publican) and fork left where the path divides, signed 'Footpath. No Cycles'. The broad track runs above and parallel with the stream. This is the infant River Derwent. It rises across the moor to the west and grows to become Derbyshire's principal river, eventually flowing into the Trent to the east of Derby.

Fork right where the path splits and walk up the side of the moor, and, where it divides again, descend briefly over a footbridge before continuing up the side, the views back towards Kinder Scout to the southwest and Bleaklow to the west becoming more impressive with every step. The path becomes smaller, and where the fence slants to the left downhill, there are gritstone rocks visible above to the northeast. Embark upon a tough and steep climb through the heather and bilberries to the single flat large rock on the edge.

A fine stroll northwest along the edge to inspect the Crow and Rocking Stones can be taken from here. Otherwise keep on due north past the rock towards the summit to see the trig point due east on the astrally named Outer Edge. Walk to that **(2)** (at 1,775ft/541m) and then head southeast following the stakes to Margery Hill, the long bulk of Kinder looming to the southwest. The path is boggy and treacherous, and when you reach the trig point on the hill you will have gained all of 16ft (5m) in height since the last! Comfort yourself with the thought that you are now 905ft (275m) above your starting point.

Howden Reservoir at King's Tree

Look south along Wilfrey and Howden Edges. The high point you see is High Stones. Head along the edge, picking up the path to High Stones **(3)**, past Featherbed Moss and Wet Stones and spy the wood in the valley to the southwest to where the route will next lead. The path descends to the line of a broken wall. Go right here and walk west down to Howden Clough, perhaps marvelling at the feat of labour it must have taken to build these walls across the moors. Take the path on the right bank which leads past a miniature reservoir, and ford the stream just before Clough Wood. At Howden Reservoir **(4)** turn right and loop back round, walking north to Slippery Stones Bridge and into Derbyshire, and then returning south to the start.

Left: Crow Stones Edge

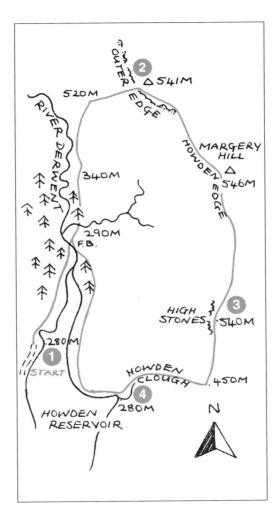

FACT FILE

Map OS Outdoor Leisure 1: The Dark Peak
Start/Finish SK 167938: the northern tip of the road leading north along the west side of Derwent and Howden Reservoirs from the A57. NB: *this road is closed to motor vehicles at weekends and on bank holidays from Good Friday until the end of October. There is a minibus service from Fairholmes*
Length 8½ miles (13.5km)
Walking time At least 5 hours
Difficulty One steep and difficult climb, and a long stretch of boggy and treacherous moor. Waterproof boots and a compass are essential. The route should not be attempted in bad weather

The Route in Brief

1 SK 167938. Walk N through the woods, cross bridge and R across next. L at path divide, R at next and down over bridge at next. Ascend path. When fence slants left downhill climb NNE to single, flat, large rock. Continue due N, and then due E to trig point.
2 SE along staked path to trig point on Margery Hill. S along edge to High Stones.
3 Along edge till descending to line of broken wall. Descend along it to clough and take path on R bank, fording stream just before wood.
4 At Howden Reservoir turn R up to bridge and then round S to start.

COWN EDGE ROCKS

This Dark Peak route begins at Rowarth village and climbs into bleak moorland country where the wind can scythe through you without mercy, and from where there are superb views not only of the surrounding countryside but also of Manchester's urban sprawl.

From the car park **(1)** (with the Little Mill Inn nearby) walk through Rowarth village and keep straight on up the track, turning left up the path signed 'Cown Edge'. Climb steeply, Kinder Scout in view to the east and the Sett valley behind to the south. At the junction of paths continue straight on north signed 'Cown Edge' again along a track leading uphill. Cross a stile over the wall at the top and keep on, following a wall to another stile and descending to Near Slack Farm **(2)**. Northwest is Manchester.

There is something uncanny about standing in beautiful country and looking down on a city.

Left: A stream in Rowarth village
Right: Hey Brows and Lantern Pike

There below is the human race with all its hopes and fears, unhappiness, desperation, joy, boredom and excitement. There are the villains and thieves, the people on the run, the girls on the streets, the huge tower blocks, the millions of phone calls and faxes, the thousands of deals, the passions and love affairs, the pubs and clubs and bright lights, the cars, buses and taxis, the distant wailing of police sirens. Up here are just the singing of a lark and the sigh of the wind.

Fork right at the farm up the path leading northeast and continue over two walls, gaining height all the time and crossing a track. There are fabulous views of the hills to the south. Cross another wall, with Cown Edge Rocks to your right. Coombes Rocks are to the left, with the line of the aptly named Mare's Back pointing down towards the curve of Coombes Edge.

Keep on past a stile on the left and a track coming in from the east. Swing to the right,

Map OS Outdoor Leisure 1: The Dark Peak
Start/Finish SK 011892: car park southwest of Rowarth
Length 5½ miles (9km)
Walking time 3 hours
Difficulty One steep climb

The Route in Brief

1 SK 011892. Through Rowarth and up track. Follow signs towards 'Cown Edge', reaching Near Slack Farm.

2 R up path, over 2 walls, a track and another wall, past rocks, a stile and track. Curve right, round hill, to meet road by house.

3 R up fenced path and branch L down to Rocks Farm. Track leads SE to road. Take path to R just before, go straight on at lane, and take path to L at bend.

4 Cross to gate and fork ½R up next field to top corner. Cross 2 fields and L up path through farm. Descend track, turning R halfway down.

5 R at track leading W past farm and over track. Do not fork R at field's end but keep on, curving down to farm and following sign back to Rowarth.

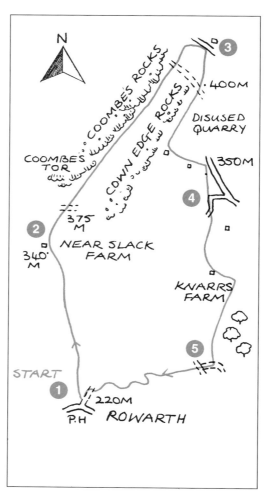

round the hill, to meet the Monk's Road on the north of the hill by a solitary house on the other side of the road **(3)**. Turn right (south) up the fenced path, reaching over 1,300ft (400m) and passing disused quarries, with wonderful southerly views that will remain with you for the rest of the route. Continue below Cown Edge Rocks and branch left down to Rocks Farm. Pass to the right of the buildings and head down and up the track leading southeast past Higher Plainstead Farm to the road.

Just before it, take the footpath to the right leading south. Keep straight on at the lane and take the footpath to the left at the bend **(4)**. Cross to the gate opposite and fork half-right up the next field, south, keeping Knarr's Nook Farm to the left, to the top corner. Carry on up two fields. New Mills is now spread out in the valley to the southwest.

Turn left up the path leading southeast through Knarr's Farm, the brown-peaked outline of The Knott (1, 490ft/454m) ahead to the east-southeast and the mass of Kinder Scout looming behind, while the views to the south continue to delight. Descend the farm track, turning right halfway down and heading south. Turn right at the farm track **(5)** leading west past Matleymoor Farm, continuing straight over at the track. Do not fork right at the end of the field but keep up the second field, eventually curving down to Higher Harthill Farm, then turning right, signed 'Rowarth', and heading west past Lower Harthill Farm, across a footbridge and back to the start.

KINDER'S NORTH EDGE

The north flank of Kinder Scout is a wonderful place to be on a fine summer's day, but can be unforgiving and threatening in bad weather. This route, on which the going can be tough, climbs very steeply to attain the superb edge which juts east from Blackden Moor towards Mill Hill, and returns to the Woodlands Valley by the Snake Path.

A path opposite the lay-by heads down and across a footbridge **(1)** over the River Ashop and then leads to the left, over a stream, and southeast up the side of the mountain, turning south to follow a broken wall up Gate Side Clough very steeply to near the summit, passing one set of rocks and continuing to another **(2)**. You are now well above 1,900ft (580m), having climbed about half that height, and can be thankful that your uphill struggle is over.

Walk in a general westerly direction along Seal and Ashop Edges for over 3½ miles (5.5km), turning south to negotiate the great rocky buttress of Fairbrook Naze about halfway along. (At this point, the last time I was there, I walked

into a freezing snow cloud, and if it hadn't been for my compass, I would probably still be there.) Along the route you will pass various interesting rock formations and ford several brooks, including Fair Brook, after which you turn south to the Naze; this can be followed as a short cut back to the valley. The going is treacherous, and it is difficult not to place at least one leg into the bog at some stage. After Fairbrook Naze the path reaches its highest point of about 2,050ft (625m), so you can fairly say you have climbed a mountain, from where you can scan the uncompromising views north over Featherbed Moss (one of several so named in the Dark Peak) towards Bleaklow. You will eventually pass to the left of the distinctively shaped rocks known as the Boxing Gloves and not too long after meet the Pennine Way on its route northwest from the Kinder Downfall.

Join it and descend steeply until you meet a stake where a sign proclaiming 'Snake Path' **(3)** directs you northwards and then east. The path may be muddling at first but soon becomes easy to make out as it follows the River Ashop, rapidly swelling in its hurry to disgorge its

Ashop Edge from the Snake Path

waters into the Ladybower Reservoir.

As Lady Clough Woods come back into view you have a choice. You can cross the river by a footbridge and continue up and down the side of Rough Bank and Nungrain Brink to the footbridge near the start. Alternatively you can remain on the north bank, following the path under Saukin Ridge either back to the footbridge or up to the main road and the pub.

Kinder Scout holds a particular fascination for me. It is the roof of the little world that is the Peak District, and always a satisfying challenge to climb for that reason. But it is also a mercurial place, inconstant, fickle and untrustworthy. I have walked along its edges in a scorching sun, while around me have sat groups of happy hikers taking their refreshment. I have also been lashed by an arctic wind and become so cold, trudging through the ice and snow, that the warmth of my car has seemed a blissful but somehow unattainable dream. It is a place to be taken seriously.

Seal Edge

Map OS Outdoor Leisure 1: The Dark Peak
Start/Finish SK 115903: small lay-by opposite start of footpath; or from the Snake Inn (if you patronise it); or from car park further up A57, walking down Lady Clough Forest Trail to river and footbridge. There are buses to the Snake Inn
Length 9 miles (14.5km)
Walking time 5 hours, more in adverse conditions
Difficulty One long very steep climb and boggy conditions. A compass is essential. Do not attempt in bad weather or when it is forecast

The Route in Brief

1 SK 115903. Path opposite lay-by leads over footbridge, L over brook and SE up side of mountain. Then N up broken wall to 2nd set of rocks near summit.
2 W along edge for 3½ miles (5.5km), round Fairbrook Naze, and NW along Pennine Way to stake signed 'Snake Path'.
3 N then E along path above Ashop River. Either cross by footbridge to S side back to footbridge near start, or continue through woods up to pub or back to footbridge.

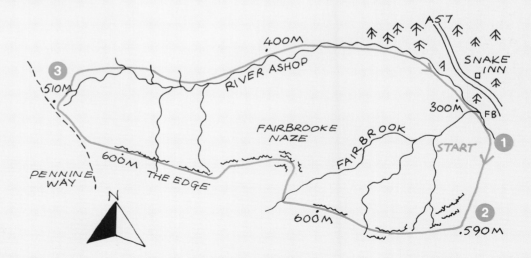

KINDER SCOUT

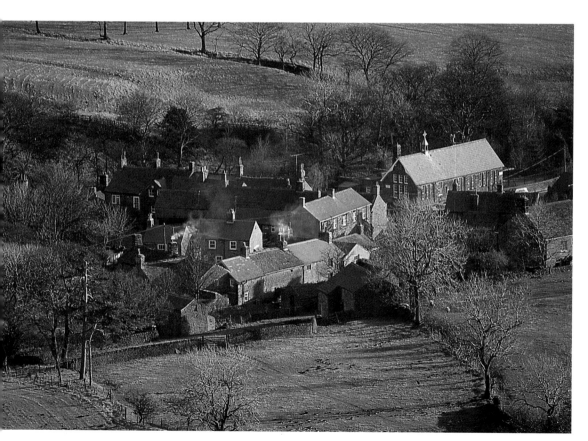

Edale Village

This exhilarating walk climbs some 1,250ft (380m) from Edale, where the Pennine Way begins, to very near the summit of Kinder Scout, the highest point in the Peak, passing on the way some fascinating rock formations and providing some superlative views. A long optional detour can be taken to the Kinder Downfall.

The village of Edale is a series of hamlets, or 'booths', dotted along the steep, dark valley. In days of old it was visited mainly by jaggers, or packhorse men, who passed through, over the footbridge we are about to cross, on their way to and from Cheshire and Yorkshire with their loads of cheese, salt and bales of wool. There are two pubs and a shop.

From the station (**1**) turn left up the lane and take the footpath north at its end. Cross the footbridge over Grinds Brook and climb the paved path through the wood. Now deviate from the obvious route and take the path straight on to the right of the mountain brook. Climb very steeply northeast up Golden Clough towards the summit. The going is slippery and tough and occasionally demanding.

At a cairn (**2**) near the top strike up half-left (northwest) and then walk west along the edge with supreme views over the Peak District. Eventually turn northwest up the clough, ford it and continue south. Ford the next major clough. Then, at some cairns, strike off to the right (west) of a much smaller stream (**3**). This path appears on the Ordnance Survey 1:25 000 map as a black dotted line. (*The green footpath on the map heads northwest to the Kinder Downfall. This is the old Pennine Way route, but it is well-nigh impassable in wet weather and difficult to follow. Those properly equipped and with a compass, however, will enjoy the challenge of crossing Edale Moor this way and returning from the Downfall along the Pennine Way to rejoin our route.*)

Pass a group of rocks and continue along the obvious path. After a second group of rocks, cairns begin to mark the route. Eventually descend to cross a clough and turn to climb southwest to almost exactly 2,000ft (610m). Continue west through the scattered rocks known as the Woolpacks, the west end of which is marked by the distinctive shape of Pym Chair, and keep on to the next landmark, the Noe Stool, passing a cairn just before it. Halfway between Pym Chair and the Noe Stool, those wishing to attain the highest point

The Moat Stone at the Woolpacks

of Kinder Scout, and therefore the Peak District, can do so by striking north of the path some 500 yards/metres, and climbing to 2,088ft (636m).

Swing southwest, joining the paved Pennine Way just before the Swine's Back (**4**). Here is another opportunity to walk to the Downfall, simply following the Pennine Way north. Otherwise descend along the Way, down Jacob's Ladder, across a footbridge, through

Lee Farm, over another footbridge, and turn up through Upper Booth farm signed 'Edale and Grindsbrook Booth'.

Another substantial climb is necessary before finally descending to Grindsbrook Booth and turning right, back to the start of the walk.

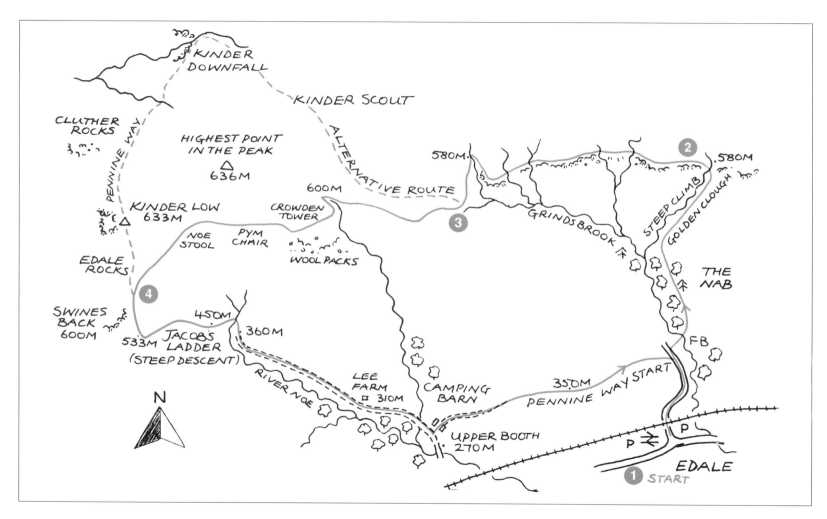

KINDER DOWNFALL

KINDER SCOUT

CLUTHER ROCKS

HIGHEST POINT IN THE PEAK
△ 636M

PENNINE WAY

ALTERNATIVE ROUTE

580M

2

580M

STEEP CLIMB

GOLDEN CLOUGH

600M

KINDER LOW 633M

CROWDEN TOWER

GRINDSBROOK

NOE STOOL

PYM CHAIR

3

WOOLPACKS

THE NAB

EDALE ROCKS

4

SWINES BACK 600M

450M

533M

JACOB'S LADDER (STEEP DESCENT)

360M

FB

N

RIVER NOE

LEE FARM
☐ 310M

CAMPING BARN

35.0M

PENNINE WAY START

P

UPPER BOOTH 270M

P

P

EDALE START

1

26

Map OS Outdoor Leisure 1: The Dark Peak
Start/Finish SK 123853: Edale station car park (charge). Edale can be reached by bus and train
Length 9½ miles (15km)
Walking time At least 5 hours
Difficulty One very steep and fairly difficult climb. A compass is essential, and do not attempt in bad weather or when it is forecast

The Route in Brief

1 SK 123853. L up lane and then paved path through wood. Straight on steeply NE up path by brook to cairn.
2 NW to summit then W along edge across 2 cloughs.
3 At cairns strike off to R (W) of small stream, pass 2 groups of rocks and follow cairns W along path, eventually swinging SW to join Pennine Way.
4 Follow Pennine Way back to Edale.

Edale, Win Hill and Lose Hill from the head of Grindsbrook Clough

MAM TOR AND THE GREAT RIDGE

This classic Dark Peak walk begins at Castleton, from where visits can be made to some of the celebrated caverns, climbs to the top of Mam Tor at just under 1,700ft (517m), then leads northeast along the back of the Great Ridge with wonderful views of the valleys of Hope and Edale below, and of Kinder Scout's brooding outline to the northwest.

Castleton has been almost smothered by the tourist trade, and the only time that it comes up for a gasp of air is on a filthy day in the depths of winter. It has to be said, however, that J. B. Firth was making similar complaints in *Highways and Byways in Derbyshire* in 1905. The village lies at the point where the limestone meets the grits and shales, where the White Peak merges into the Dark, and is surrounded by hills, gorges, caves and underground caverns of all shapes and sizes.

The main reason for its popularity are the four caverns that can be visited by the public. All are of great interest, and my own particular favourite is the Speedwell Cavern, an old lead mine. Here you are pushed along the level in a boat to see the Bottomless Pit, which used to fascinate and haunt me as a child. An earlier visitor to Castleton was Lord Byron. He and Mary Chaworth were punted through the remarkable Peak Cavern; but love, not geological wonders, were foremost in the poet's mind. 'The Companion of my transit,' he wrote, 'was M.A.C., with whom I had long been in love and never told it, though she had discovered it without. I recollect my sensations but cannot describe them, and it is as well.'

From the car park **(1)**, from which there is a good view of Peveril Castle (see Walk 14), cross the road and go down the little street opposite signposted 'Riverside Walk to Peak Cavern'. Follow the stream, turn right into the road, cross the bridge and go up Goosehill. Continue along the track which leads through the gate and along the wall in a westerly direction to the Speedwell Cavern **(2)**. The Cavern stands at the entrance to Winnats Pass. This spectacularly steep, rocky and wind-channelling gorge was for many

centuries the main route east to Castleton, and was much used by packhorse trains carrying salt from Cheshire to Sheffield. When the A625 round Mam Tor, built on unstable foundations, collapsed, it once again became the only route in from the west.

Cross the road to the car park and climb a stile, then another in the opposite corner of the field. Now go straight on northwest along the line of the wall to join a concrete path leading up to Treak Cliff Cavern, where remains of Bronze Age Man were found, and continue past the buildings on a path which winds round and up the hillside, giving extensive views back beyond Castleton and of the Odin Mine, one of the oldest lead mines in the Peak, below to the north.

Continue over a wide wooden stile to the Blue John Cavern (3), where once the famous mineral was mined in quantity. Turn right at the entrance up the little road and take a detour right at the road to view the sheer face of Mam Tor – 'mother mountain'.

Now retrace your steps, past the little road to the Blue John Mine and almost as far as the junction of roads. Here climb the stile in the wall on the right, signposted 'NT path to Mam Tor', and climb steeply to the summit, following dark-green-tipped posts and then stone steps. The views from the top are

Opposite: The Great Ridge
Right: Looking back to Mam Tor

superb. A hillfort and settlement was built here by the Celts before the Iron Age, which at 16 acres (6.5ha) was the largest in Derbyshire. It must have been well-nigh impregnable, and its defenders are more likely to have died from the cold than the enemy's spear.

Now walk the couple of miles (3 km) northeast along the Great Ridge past Hollins Cross and Back Tor to Lose Hill, which stands at 1,563ft (475m) **(4)**. You are likely to meet other walkers along this popular route, and erosion has become a problem in places. However, the overwhelming sensation is one of solitude and peace.

Leave Lose Hill half-right, walking south-southwest down a stone-surfaced path and, after a stile and at a cairn, taking a path on the right side of a broken wall. Now follow footpath signs to Castleton, turning right at the first, crossing a stile and turning right over a double stile at another, then crossing a field to another stile and taking the farm road. Cross a stile, again signed 'Castleton', where the road turns at a right angle down to a farm. Harebells and foxgloves thrive here in the summer months. Turn left at a stile down another farm road, then left over a stile by a footpath sign along the edge of a field, down some steps, across a footbridge over a brook and left along the edges of two fields.

Castleton

Turn right at the lane past nineteenth-century Losehill Hall (5), now the National Park Study Centre. Where the lane bends to the left, go straight ahead over a stile. Castleton is now in view. Keep to the right edge of the field and cross the next stile and field, keeping to the left of the barn. Head left down the track, left again at Hollowford Road and back into the village near Peveril Castle.

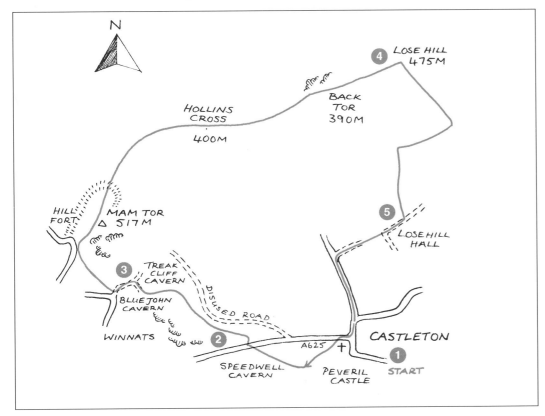

FACT FILE

Map OS Outdoor Leisure 1: The Dark Peak
Start/Finish SK 149830: there are train stations at nearby Hope and Edale, connecting with Manchester, Sheffield and elsewhere, and there are buses to Castleton from a wide variety of places
Length 6½ miles (10.5km)
Walking time 4 hours. Allow a day or more if you wish to visit any of the caverns
Difficulty Generally easy, though the climb up Mam Tor is steep

The Route in Brief

1 SK 149830. Leave village by Goosehill and take path WSW then ENE to Speedwell Cavern.
2 Cross road and take path N, then NW to Treak Cliff Cavern. Wind round and up hillside to Blue John Cavern.
3 At entrance turn R up road. Divert to see face of Mam Tor. Otherwise turn L down road and R at footpath to Mam Tor summit. Then NW turning NNW along Great Ridge 2 miles (3 km) to Lose Hill.
4 Leave summit ½R, SSE, down path. At cairn take path to R of broken wall. Follow signs towards Castleton.
5 R at lane past Losehill Hall, straight ahead at stile, across fields, L down track and L at Hollowford Road back to Castleton.

STANAGE EDGE

The walk along Stanage Edge is one of the most glorious and splendid in the Peak. The route begins at the village of Hathersage, climbs Bole Hill and crosses wild moorland before returning along the Edge and down through pleasing farmland.

The attractive gritstone village of Hathersage was once a smoky place where several mills were busy producing needles and buttons and drawing wire. It was also traditionally where millstones were made. Many can be seen abandoned on the hillsides where they were fashioned. It is from the Iron Age that the fort of Carl Wark dates. It lies above and east of the village and is easily reached by footpaths.

The village has fascinating connections with the legend of Robin Hood. Various places in England claim to have been his territory, but if ever there really was such a man, then the hills and moors around Hathersage are most likely to have been his stamping ground.

The evidence, such as it is, is this. Loxley, where he is said to have been born, is less than seven miles (11km) away across country, now half swallowed up by Sheffield. In 1637 a survey for the Earl of Arundel's estate records a field at Loxley 'wherein is ye foundacion of an house or Cottage where Robin Hood was borne'. The country between, with its cave systems and vantage points, is perfect as a refuge for an outlaw band. A brook we are about to cross is even called the Hood, and the earliest versions of the tale place Robin and his men in the nearby Forest of Barnsdale rather than Sherwood Forest. There is also a 10ft-long (3m) grave near the south porch of the church which has always been reputed to be that of Little John.

Elias Ashmole, the seventeenth-century antiquary who founded the Ashmolean Museum in Oxford, visited the church and recorded the strong local tradition. Tantalisingly, he writes of seeing a longbow, said to be Little John's, hanging in the church. It was made of yew, over 6ft (2m) long and required immense strength to draw it. It subsequently disappeared. In 1784 the grave was opened and a thigh-bone which measured

Stormy day on Stanage Edge

30in (75cm) taken out and later reburied. It could only belong to a giant well over 7ft (2.2m) tall. Moreover, in the church porch is a medieval gravestone said to be the original one from the grave. It bears the initials 'J.L.' for John Little. Call me fanciful if you like, but to me this is Robin Hood's home countryside and refuge. Local tradition very often has at least one foot in fact, and it has always been too strong around Hathersage to be entirely discounted.

Facing the handsome church from the little car park to its north (1), walk up its right side, turn right along the wall and follow the path down to a lane. Turn right, pass the cricket pitch and cross the field on the left after 'Riverside' diagonally to a footbridge across the Hood Brook. Turn right along the track, shortly fork left (northwest) and climb fairly steeply through Cliff Wood.

Halfway up the hillside to the northeast can be seen North Lees Hall, on the site of one of seven large houses in the area said to have been originally built within sight of one another by Robert Eyre, whose father fought at Agincourt, for his seven sons. The ancient family of Eyre held sway in these parts for many centuries. The church has several fine memorials to them, including Robert and Joan and their 14 children. Another of the Eyre houses was on the site of Brookfield Manor, which can be seen down in the valley after you climb a stile. Walk round and up past Birley Farm, turn left into Birley Lane (2) and then right into Cogger's Lane. The views from here are extensive across the Hope valley to the moors and hills around, marred only by the cement works outside Castleton, and to Bamford Edge above to the northwest.

Take the bridleway towards 'Hurst Clough and Bamford' shortly on the left and head northwest down a line of hawthorns and then a hedge after a gate. Cross the brook and begin to climb, The Tower visible behind. Pass to the left of Nether Hurst Farm (3) and up an old muddy track, turning right into Hurstclough Lane at a junction, Win Hill (1,516ft/462m) showing itself to the northwest. Carry on as another track comes in from the right and pass the drive to Upper Hurst Farm. Take the path on the left as the lane bends down to the right. Head north, climbing up the large field to a stile in the belt of trees. Follow the 'Bamford Road' path northwest, now descending to cross the Upper Hurst Brook (4).

Climb and take the track on the right, northeast turning north across the open moor, Stanage Edge now standing proudly to the east. At an eerie heather-clad disused quarry head due north to a point midway between two small rocky outcrops to find a deteriorating double wall. From here make your way north-northeast to the Edge (5). (The official footpath goes quite far north to join another leading south past the Boundary Stones marking Derbyshire's border with Yorkshire.)

Walk south and southeast along the Edge, following the Roman route of the Long Causeway. The views northwest are stupendous, over the pointed pikes of Win Hill and Lose Hill (1,563ft/475m) to the great mass of Kinder Scout behind. Hathersage lies to the south in the valley below. The trig point you reach marks High Neb, the summit of the Edge at 1,502ft (458m) and the path below is strewn with abandoned millstones. The tower blocks of Sheffield break the eastern skyline in a strange contrast to the massive open spaces.

Cross a stile and branch right not long after, forking right again and descending a marvellous and ancient paved track known as Jacob's Ladder which leads through a wood. Keep left when the path splits to reach a road. East of here, under the Edge, is Robin Hood's Cave, where several caves and passages would have provided a perfect hideout for the outlaw. Turn left at the road and shortly right past a hut to descend southwest along the brook and past North Lees Hall to a lane.

North Lees was built by William Jessop, possibly to a design by Robert Smythson. Charlotte Brontë visited Hathersage to stay with friends at the Vicarage in 1845, and it is thought that she made North Lees the model for Thornfield in *Jane Eyre*, which she completed two years later, borrowing the name of the once dominant local family for her heroine. In more ways than one, Hathersage is

North Lees Hall and Brookfield Manor below the Edge

Map OS Pathfinder 743: Sheffield
Start/Finish SK 234818: little car park behind (north of) the church. Hathersage can be easily reached by train or bus
Length 10 miles (16km)
Walking time 5½ hours
Difficulty A compass is essential for the moorland navigation

The Route in Brief

1 SK 234818. Facing church from car park, go into graveyard, R along wall, R at lane, diagonally L after 'Riverside' to footbridge, R at track, shortly fork L (NW) up through wood and past farm to lane.
2 L, R at junction, L down bridle road across brook and up to farm.
3 Up track and R into lane. L at path as descending lane bends to R. N to trees and NW along path for Bamford Road. L over brook.
4 R over track NE and N across moor. N at quarry, heading to between 2 stony outcrops to double wall. NNE to Edge.
5 S and SE along Edge till R soon after stile down paved path through wood. Keep L as path splits. L at road, R past hut, past Hall to lane.
6 L across brook, R along path over pasture, across brook and up to church.

the model for the village of Morton in the book (Morton too being a local name). There is also some evidence that Moorseats, yet another Eyre house just north of Hathersage, was the model for Moor House, the home of the ghastly St John Rivers. Go left across the brook **(6)** and right along a path, Brookfield Manor to the right, past Cowclose Farm and over the pastures, heading down across a brook and back to the church, gaining a glimpse of Moorseats in the trees to the north-northeast as you do so.

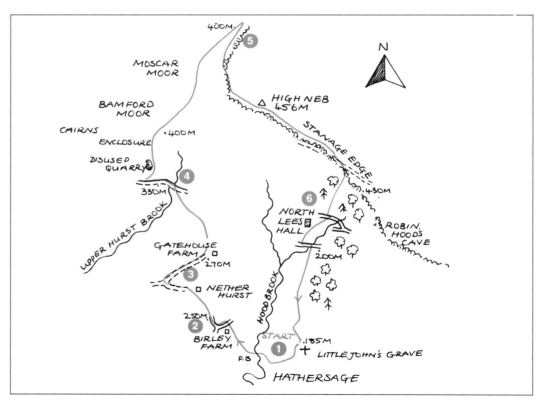

MILLTHORPE

This most easterly of the walks in this book is a quietly satisfying exploration of the district south of the village of Millthorpe, taking in dale and top, woodland and pasture, all in deep country which belies its proximity to the built-up areas of Dronfield and Chesterfield.

From the centre of Millthorpe **(1)** (where there are two pubs), go down Mill Lane, cross the brook, cross the stile ahead at the entrance to Mill Farm and walk south over the next brook. Cross a stile and turn left (south) to the right of a hedge, over a stile, and up, keeping to the left of the next hedge. Barlow Woodseats Hall can be glimpsed to the left. This attractive gabled building was built by Arthur Mower in the seventeenth century around an older house. Turn right through a gateway and walk along a hedge and over a field into Rose Wood **(2)**.

Go straight over a riding track and curve left downhill to cross a brook. Turn left just before the edge of the wood and continue through it. Take the wider of two paths which head back into its midst and walk south, crossing a brook

North to Totley Moor from Grange Lumb Farm

and then a larger one, and heading steeply up and out. Keep south, crossing the brook again, up across the fields to Moorhall **(3)**.

Pass to the right of the buildings and walk up the lane to the road. Go left and right over

a stile at Bank Farm. Now follow the path south-southeast across the fields, down through Grange Wood and across the brook,

Map OS Outdoor Leisure 24: The White Peak
Start/Finish SK 317764: Millthorpe. There are buses to Millthorpe from Holmesfield, Chesterfield and elsewhere
Length 5¾ miles (9km)
Walking time 3 hours
Difficulty Easy going

The Route in Brief

1 SK 317764. Down Mill Lane, over brook, over stile at entrance to Mill Farm, over next brook and stile and L up hedge. Over stile, up hedge, and R through gateway to wood.

2 Over track, L over brook, and L at edge of wood. Take wider of 2 paths into wood, over 2 brooks, out of wood, and S over brook and fields to Moorhall.

3 Up lane to road. L and R over stile. Follow path SSE to Grange Lumb Farm, on over road, up road past Barlow Grange, across B6050, down track ahead, R along path, cross wall, past house and E to Cow Close Farm.

4 R at road, L at lane by inn, L down path well before house, L up bridleway, R over stile, across brook, past holiday homes, up fields, R at green lane, L and R at road, and down past reservoir.

5 R and L at road, over brook, up pasture, across 2 roads and take sunken lane back to start.

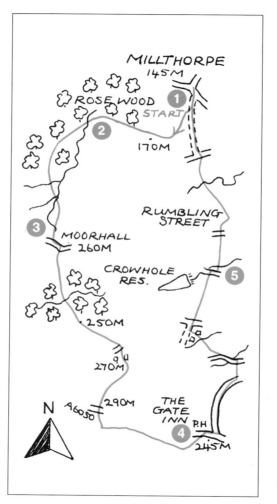

where there is an ancient feeling, and up past Grange Lumb Farm, keeping in the same direction through a gap in the holly hedge and on, southeast. Cross the road and walk up the road ahead past Barlow Grange, across the B6050 and down the track ahead. Chesterfield is visible in the east. Swing right off the track along a footpath, crossing a wall, and down past Bluster Castle, turning east towards Cow Close Farm. Turn right at the road.

The Gate Inn is a free house, well positioned at about half distance. Turn left down the lane by it **(4)** and, one field before the house on the left, turn left down the path left of the wall. Turn left up the public bridleway after the brook and, after about 150 yards/metres, right by the stile by the gate. Follow the path down across a brook and up past a neat complex of holiday homes, wallabies and all. Now climb the pasture, turning right at a wide green lane. The rest of the walk is northerly. Reach a farm and walk through the yard, turning left and immediately right at the road **(5)**. Descend the pastures, Crowhole Reservoir to the left. The stone round here has a honey-coloured tinge to it, rather like that of the Cotswolds. At the next road go right and immediately left, over a brook and steeply up the pasture along a hedge. Cross the next road at Rumbling Street and go down the track, across a brook and through a wood. Go over the road at Johnnygate and descend by the old sunken lane to the brook and back to the start.

BIRCHEN AND BASLOW EDGES

The sequence of high edges that extends down the Peak District's eastern side is a delight to walker and climber alike. This route visits two of them, passes some curious rock formations and crosses a wild tract of moor.

Cross the road **(1)** and head south through the gate along a path signed 'Open Country' and across an ancient burial ground strewn with rocks. Baslow Edge runs alongside to the east, and Curbar village is to the west. Pass through a gateway in a wall and eventually pick up a track leading down to Lady Wall Well on the edge of Baslow (where there are shops and pubs), the Derwent valley laid out ahead. Chatsworth is due south, out of sight.

Just after a trough turn left up a track past the well and shortly fork left (north) up another, often muddy, track. To the east are the rocks of Gardom's Edge. Cross the boundary into Open Country **(2)** and fork right up the wall, Wellington's Monument in view ahead. Descend through boulders, oaks and birches, east turning southeast. Cross a stile at the boundary of the Open Country and keep on down, probably very muddily, across a footbridge over the Bar Brook to the road. Cross and climb south then southeast through birch woods to the southern tip of Gardom's Edge, where Birchen Edge comes into view to the east. Nelson's Monument stands out to the northeast as you descend gently through bracken to the road.

Turn left and shortly fork left past the Robin Hood Inn **(3)**, soon bearing left again after a house, over a stile into Access Land. Keep left, straight on north, following the wall and then the track as the fence jinks away from it. Keep left at the first fork and right at the second. Just

Gibbet Moor from Birchen Edge

Map OS Outdoor Leisure 24: The White Peak
Start/Finish SK 259748: lay-by on left on the road running east from Curbar just before the sign saying 'P 200 yds'. There are buses to Curbar from Baslow, which is accessible from many places
Length 6¾ miles (11km)

Walking time 3½ hours
Difficulty Easy going. A compass would be handy

The Route in Brief

1 SK 259748. Cross road and head S to Lady Wall Well. L up track and fork L to Open Country.
2 R up wall and descend past Open Country boundary, over brook to road. Cross and climb S and SE, then descend to road. Turn L to inn.
3 Fork L and L again past house into Access Land. N to Nelson's Monument and on across moor to road junction. L after stile, cross road, then road bridge.
4 Ascend, L into Open Country, and W and SW to Wellington's Monument. R at junction of paths to road and L to lay-by.

past Nelson's Monument to the right above, climb the short distance up to the Edge by whichever path you fancy.

The monument, a plain gritstone column, was built by John Brightman, a Baslow man, in 1810, long before the rather grander one in Trafalgar Square. Nearby are three rocks named after three of Nelson's ships, *Victory*, *Defiance* and *Royal Soverin*. In the old days there were various superstitions attached to this place, and the locals were not keen to tread the path we have just taken, but now we rejoin it to head north to the road junction across the moor which is littered with relics of ancient times.

This part of the walk can be a chilly affair when an unkind wind is blowing from the north. At the junction turn left after the ladder stile, cross the road, and then the road bridge over the brook **(4)**. Climb the road and turn left through a gate into Open Country, taking the track which leads west then southwest to Wellington's Monument, a 10ft-high (3m) cross erected in 1866 to celebrate the victor of Waterloo. At the junction of paths turn right and head north past the Eagle Stone. This remnant of a harder band of rock was regarded as sacred by earlier civilisations and is said to turn round at cock-crow. At the road, with Curbar Edge stretching ahead, turn left back to the lay-by.

CHATSWORTH AND HADDON

This fairly long and satisfying route not only visits two of the great houses of Derbyshire but also offers the walker a good variety of scenery and terrain, from parkland to woodland, from ancient tracks to a disused railway line, from glimpses of wild moorland to the comparative lushness of the valleys of the Derwent and the Wye.

Edensor (pronounced 'Enzer') is one of several villages and hamlets on the vast Chatsworth estate and was mostly built (in many different styles) around 1840 when it was moved from along the river. There are a couple of shops. The church contains a very fine monument to the sons of Bess of Hardwick, and the churchyard contains several noteworthy graves.

Leave the village **(1)** and turn right down the B6012. At the bend fork left and climb the bank ahead, following an indistinct path leading southeast towards the Derwent. There are fine views of the house and the Hunting Tower above. Whole books have been written about Chatsworth. The principal seat of the Duke of Devonshire is one of the great houses and treasure troves of Britain, indeed Europe. Suffice it to say that the visitor should allow at least a day to view the house and its equally splendid gardens. The Duke is a friend to the walker and allows access to thousands of his acres.

Do not quite reach the river, but slightly downstream from the first weir fork half-right (south), walking about halfway up the bank above the river. Beeley Moor looms above to the southeast. The path meets the road again. Cross it and turn left, passing through the gate and taking the lane past the car park and sawmill **(2)**.

Follow the lane round and turn hard left down over the brook and up past Calton Lees Farm. Fork left at the end of the road, following the path south down the meadows to the river again. Lindop Wood covers the hillside to the west, while the floor of the valley must be as flat as anywhere in the Peak. Meet the river and veer away again over a stile by a gate into Bank Wood, where the going may be muddy, and out again, swinging southwest along a wall and then, very muddily, the river,

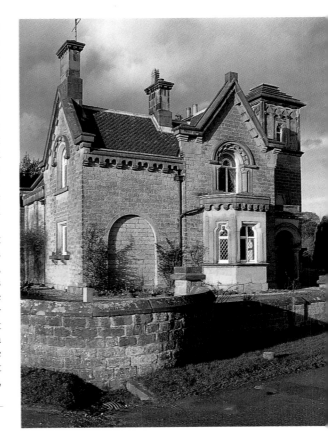

Eccentric architecture in Edensor

41

the houses of Rowsley now in view. The Peacock Inn here is famous. It was built as a private house in 1652 and, like most of the village, is owned by the Duke of Rutland as part of the Haddon estate. The rivers Wye and Derwent meet just south of the village. There are two or three shops and the church contains the exquisite tomb of the 23-year-old Catherine Manners.

Pass under the disused railway bridge **(3)**, turn right at the road and walk north out of the village, continuing northwest up a track to Bouns Corner Wood. This would once have been the old route to Bakewell, and it is difficult not to compare old and new with depressing results as one looks down with distaste at the traffic on the A6. The walled track turns north, skirting the wood, then heads west, forking left into the wood, with conifers to the left and sycamores to the right, past a clearing. Emerge and continue west, with fine views south to Stanton Moor and beyond. Go straight where three tracks meet, signed 'Bakewell via Haddon'. The old road to Bakewell is the middle route, with the town now visible in the distance. The junction evokes visions of the many mules, carts, horses, coaches and carriages that must have passed this way over the centuries, some bearing the local folk to market, others carrying princes, kings and queens. Fork right

Chatsworth

at the next junction, keeping west and then southwest past Bowling Green Farm (4).

Keep straight along the bridleway as a private track goes off to the right, and turn right along the iron fence of Haddon Hall. Continue westerly through two gates. Bakewell church comes into view ahead and there are fine old trees in the park on the left. Follow the fence down and round to the corner of the field and go through the third gate. Descend to the Wye (5), a gorgeous river, healthy weed growing below the clear blue-green water. Turn left along it before the bridge and over another for an excursion to the Hall, walking a short distance along the road to the entrance gates.

Haddon is one of the most romantic houses in Britain and is the Derbyshire seat of the Duke of Rutland. It was left practically empty for nearly 300 years until the 1920s, thus escaping Georgian and Victorian 'improvements', and is certainly one of the finest of all medieval houses. It can be satisfactorily visited in an afternoon.

Retrace your steps to the second of the bridges if you have made the detour. Either way take the path signed 'Coombes Road' before the bridge leading north, parallel with the river. At the end of a wood of willows turn right up the fence to a stile under a lovely mixed wood, sycamores predominating. Now head north (left) up the track to join the Monsal Trail, part of the former Midland Railway, by crossing the lane. Head northwest to east of Bakewell.

Just after a bridge (6) climb steps to the right and take a broad green path east up over a golf course and steeply through Manners Wood, following the brook and heading east. Emerge at the top of the escarpment and walk east across Calton Pastures, Gibbet and Beeley Moors rising to the east. Gibbet Moor is said to have been given its sinister name after an incident when a tramp who had killed a woman in her cottage was gibbeted alive there.

By a pond keep on towards Chatsworth, walking east-southeast downhill, the conifers of New Piece Wood to the left and keeping left of Calton Plantations ahead. The green track, broad by now, swings north through New Piece Wood by a Dutch barn, signed 'Edensor and Chatsworth'. Now keep on north-northeast with terrific views of the house, accompanied by the Hunting Tower on the hill behind to its north, and the fountain to its south. Beyond are the moors and, behind to the north, tree-lined Curbar Edge. Head for the spire of Edensor church and back to the start.

Edensor church and village, the Hunting Tower behind

Map OS Outdoor Leisure 24: The White Peak
Start/Finish SK 251699: Edensor, which can be reached by bus
Length 9 miles (14.5km)
Walking time 4 hours. Allow far more if you wish to visit Chatsworth and/or Haddon
Difficulty Easy walking

The Route in Brief

1 SK 251699. From Edensor, R at B6012, L at bend and SE through park almost to river, then S to meet road again. Cross and L through gate to sawmill.
2 Follow lane round and L over brook. L up footpath and S down to river, through wood and on to railway bridge.
3 R on to road and N out of village, taking track through wood. Straight on at junction signed 'Bakewell via Haddon' and R at next junction to farm.
4 Straight along bridleway, R along park fence and through 3rd gate down to river.
5 L for excursion to Haddon, otherwise R on bend before river towards Coombs Road and R up fence. L at track to join Monsal Trail, heading NW.
6 Leave trail after bridge, crossing golf course and heading E up through wood and across pastures, following signs to Chatsworth to return to Edensor.

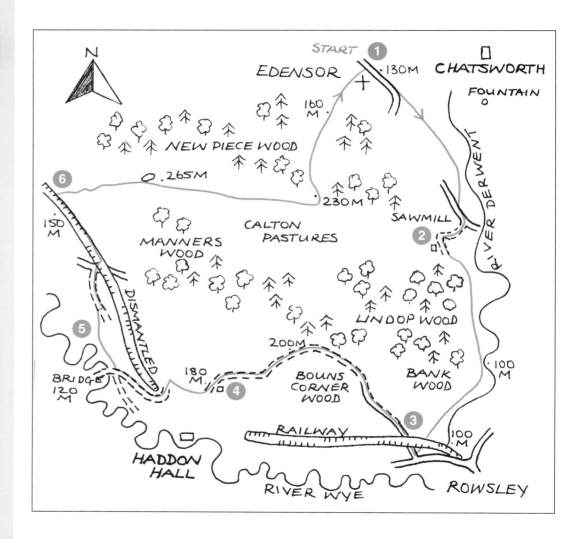

HARTHILL MOOR

Harthill Moor, like its near neighbour Stanton Moor, is studded with intriguing sites, in this case an ancient fort, a stone circle, a hermit's cave and some extraordinary rock formations. The route leads from the village of Elton north to the River Bradford at Youlgreave, then back over this fascinating territory.

Elton is a thriving community built on the spring line between the limestone and the gritstone, as the buildings south and north of the road demonstrate. The pub, the Duke of York, is extremely rewarding, especially if you are lucky enough to find it open. The route begins at the church **(1)**. Go down Well Street and take the concrete paved lane to the left. Go through the gate and take the path ahead down the narrow field, Anthony Hill rising to 961ft (293m) ahead. Cross a stile at the bottom of the valley and climb up to a lane and on to the summit. From here you can see the distinctive gritstone formation of Robin Hood's Stride, also known as Mock Beggars' Hall, to the northeast, and beyond and above it Stanton Moor, with

Birchover nestling below it to the east (see Walk 13). Due north in the distance is Youlgreave, with Over Haddon above it.

Descend past Cliff Farm **(2)** and skirt Tomlinson Wood. At a gateway fork left (northwest), to 'Hopping Farm' and 'Middleton', and walk up the meadows to the west end of Bleakley Plantation. Keep straight on (west) at the track, with Youlgreave now below and Over Haddon above it. Stanton in Peak is behind to the east-northeast. Hopping Farm appears below, with Lomberdale Hall in the distance below the woods to the northwest (see Walk 28). Descend to the farm **(3)**, crossing a lane, and continue towards Middleton Dale.

Just over a well-made wall near the bottom of the valley turn right (northeast) along the line of telephone wires to a stile in the wall. Continue, with disused Mawstone Mine visible on the ridge to the southeast, past the hump of Wenley Hill. Reach the bank of the River Bradford (see Walk 28) and descend to the road bridge. Turn right and take the path on the left marked 'Limestone Way' **(4)**.

Cross the meadows and Bleakley Dike and ascend to the gorsey bank, taking the track to the gate the other side. Take the path ahead for 'Robin Hood's Stride', cutting up the side of a hill upon which Castle Ring, an Iron Age

The Hermit's Cave

fort, sits in a commanding position. Pass to the right of Harthill Moor Farm **(5)**. Robin Hood's Stride, or Mock Beggars' Hall, comes into view to the south-southeast and Stanton Moor to the east. Reach a lane. Almost due east is Nine Stones stone circle. There are only four stones now, with a fifth acting as a gatepost to the south, but there were still seven early last century. It may be that the two stone 'chimneys' of Mock Beggars' Hall were used to study the movements of the sun, moon and

45

stars from it. Ahead to the southeast is Cratcliffe Tor.

The path continues southeast. Spare some time to investigate the Stride, from which there are excellent views northeast towards Haddon and Chatsworth, and then deviate east (6) to visit the Hermit's Cave on the south side of the Tor (from which there is a fine view of Stanton Hall, home of the Thornhill family, to the north-northeast). This extraordinary dwelling has a crucifix carved out of the stone and a niche for a lamp, both of which might be 700 years old. It is likely that more than one hermit has lived here down the centuries. It was certainly occupied in 1549, for the records of Haddon Hall mention a payment 'unto ye harmytt for ye brengynge of V Coppull of Counys [ten rabbits] from Bradley to Haddon'. The yew tree outside the cave enhances the religious feeling of the spot.

All these exciting places lie just off the Portway, an ancient track that runs north to south through Derbyshire, and it is along its route that we now continue, descending south to meet a track. At the end of the track ascend the steep lane ahead. Pass between two houses and take a path to the right over a stile some 200 yards/metres further on opposite the disused Portaway (Portway) Mine in the trees to the left. This sometimes indistinct path leads southwest back up to Elton church.

The stone circle on Harthill Moor

FACT FILE

Map OS Outdoor Leisure 24: The White Peak
Start/Finish SK 223609: Elton church. There are buses to Elton
Length 5¾ miles (9km)
Walking time 4 hours, but longer if you wish to take your time exploring some of the sites along the route
Difficulty Two or three decent ascents

The Route in Brief

1 SK 223609. From church go down Well St and take paved path to L. Through gate and take path ahead down narrow field. Traverse valley, crossing lane to summit on other side and descending to Cliff Farm.
2 Pass farm, skirt wood, and take path signed 'Hopping Farm', keeping straight on at track and descending to farm.
3 Continue towards Middleton Dale, turning R near valley bottom and following telephone wires to stile. Walk NE to River Bradford road bridge, turn R and go L signed 'Limestone Way'.
4 SSE to pass Castle Ring, signed 'Robin Hood's Stride'.

5 SE past Harthill Moor Farm to Robin Hood's Stride.
6 Detour to Hermit's Cave, then S to meet track, then steep lane. R at stile 200 yards/metres past houses and SW to Elton.

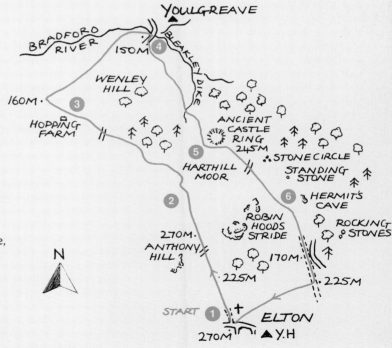

47

STANTON MOOR

Left: North over Carrs Wood
Opposite: Winster from Wyn's Tor

Stanton Moor is one of the most exciting and unusual places in the Peak District. The Nine Ladies Stone Circle is an important and well-preserved site, and the moor is littered with other relics of early man. The walk presents few difficulties, leading uphill from the ancient village of Winster to the Moor, and returning past Rowtor Rocks and along the route of an Iron Age road.

Winster is an attractive old lead mining village with various interesting buildings. The Hall was once the home of the antiquary Llewellyn Jewitt. The forecourt is said to be haunted by a white lady, a daughter of the house who leapt to her death from the parapet with her lover. There are two useful grocer's shops in the village.

From the ancient Market House in the centre of the village, the first property to be acquired by the National Trust in Derbyshire (in 1906) **(1)**, descend Woodhouse Lane opposite, north towards Birchover, passing through a gate and a stile. A partly paved track leads down to the valley bottom over Millclose Brook and up the other side, forking right, Northeast then north, and climbing more steeply up through a stile in the wall and then another. Pass mine spoil on the left and reach the summit, Stanton Moor visible ahead. Continue past a farm on the left and a mound with a capped 400ft (122m) deep mine shaft. Cross Clough Lane **(2)** and head up the field through the next stile and on to Barn Farm.

Go through the stile ahead at the crosspaths and turn immediately right along the fence to the stile by the gate. Follow round to the left onto a track leading to a stile by a gate. Now keep to the right-hand fence, overlooking Sabine Hay Wood and across Darley Dale to the east. Go through the stile to the right of the gate and cut across the corner of the field up to the footpath sign at the minor road **(3)**. Riber Castle, built by John Smedley in the 1860s but now gutted, can be plainly seen standing at some 850ft (260m) east-southeast above Matlock Bath.

Turn left, then shortly right by the National Trust sign 'Stanton Moor Edge' up the track. This is Stanton Moor, an extraordinary plateau of millstone grit at some 1,000ft (305m), marooned in a sea of softer rock. Heather and wild bilberries grow thickly, and there are several large gritstone outcrops and solitary stones. Walk round the edge of the moor, northeast, then north-northeast, passing the Cat Stone, then the Reform Tower, which was built by the Thornhills of Stanton Hall to celebrate the passing of the Reform Bill in 1832. Go through a stile in a fence and turn left down the track. You will shortly come across the Nine Ladies Stone Circle.

Stanton Moor is riddled with burial chambers and other sites dating from the Bronze Age. It was excavated earlier this century by the father and son team of J. & J. P. Heathcote of Birchover. There were many exciting finds, including several interments with axe-heads, knives, beads and urns. There are various stone circles, of which the Nine Ladies is the most obvious. Thirty-five feet (10.5m) in diameter, it has another, leaning, standing stone – the King's Stone – some way away to the southwest. It is a magical spot, and the walker should linger or at least allow time to explore the rest of this remarkable little moor.

Continue south-southwest till turning right (west) at the path intersection, passing the Cork Stone (4), and descending off the moor to the road. Notice the Andle Stone in a field across the road to the northwest. Turn left, then right into the big lay-by opposite the quarry and down a lovely track southwest through the woods to Birchover.

Emerge at the road, cross it and take the track leading down west by the side of the Druid Inn

Map OS Outdoor Leisure 24: The White Peak
Start/Finish SK 242605: Winter, which can be reached by bus
Length 6 miles (9.5km)
Walking time 3½ hours. Allow much longer if you wish to explore Stanton Moor, Rowtor Rocks, Winster and Birchover
Difficulty Fairly easy walking

The Route in Brief

1 SK 242605. Descend Woodhouse Lane towards Birchover opposite Market House. Cross to other side of valley, forking R NE then north and continue up to and across lane.
2 Continue N to Barn Farm, turning R along fence and L on to track, and on up to minor road.
3 L and R at NT sign 'Stanton Moor Edge'. Track leads round edge of moor
past Cat Stone and Reform Tower. L down track after stile, past Stone Circle
and R (W) at path intersection to Cork Stone.
4 Descend W off moor, L at road, R in lay-by and SW through wood to Birchover. Track by Druid Inn leads

W; straight on at hairpin bend and follow edge of wood W, turning SSW across pasture to road.
5 Cross road and field, L into Dudwood Lane, ascend to road and on SSE past Grey Tor. L at road and at junction E up track on R. L opposite and past Wyn's Tor back to Winster.

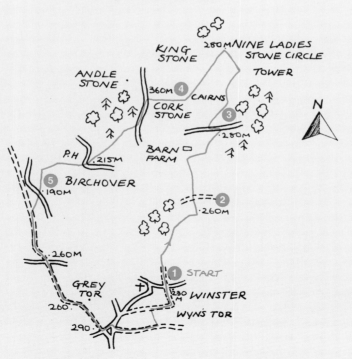

(there is another pub and a shop in the village). Almost immediately on the right are the Rowtor Rocks, which must be explored. Rising 150ft (45m), they owe their present shapes, steps, rooms, chairs and alcoves to the efforts of Thomas Eyre, a clergyman who lived nearby in Rowtor Hall (on which site the Vicarage now stands) and who died in 1717. He fashioned them into a wonderfully eccentric retreat for himself and his friends. They afford good views to the north and west.

At a hairpin bend to the left in the track keep straight on towards a gate, following the grassy track to the left just before it. Then take the left-hand of two gates, following the edge of the wood. There are splendid views of Robin Hood's Stride, also known as Mock Beggars' Hall because of its two rock 'chimneys' (see Walk 12), and Cratcliffe Rocks. Continue along a partly paved track south-southwest down the pasture to a stile over a brook. Climb to the road **(5)** and cross to the stile opposite. Cross the field and turn left into Dudwood Lane.

We now head almost due south along the very ancient route, perhaps Iron Age in origin, known as the Portway. Follow it as it climbs steeply up the minor road, crosses and continues past Grey Tor. Turn left at the road and, at the junction, head east up the farm track on the right. Go left at the stile opposite tree-clad Wyn's Tor, which you pass on the left, and descend to a stile at the bottom, turning right through some attractive hillside cottages back to the start.

CAVE DALE AND PEVERIL CASTLE

This route passes the entrance to Peveril Castle with an opportunity to visit it, and then makes use of the Limestone Way to rise south from Castleton up Cave Dale and explore the exposed and bleak high ground above, which is pitted and scarred with hundreds of disused lead mines, before returning with splendid views of the castle and village.

From the car park **(1)** turn left and then right opposite the Bull's Head. Go left across the Market Square to Bargate and follow the sign to 'Cave Dale and Limestone Way'. The opportunity to visit Peveril Castle should not be missed, though English Heritage's admission hut blocking the approach is a depressing sight. How much more romantic it was when you were able to scramble up to it unhindered and uncharged, feeling as though you had made an exciting discovery.

The castle, of course, gave the village its name. It was built by William Peveril, bastard son of William the Conqueror, and added to by Henry II, who had confiscated it from Peveril's grandson for cuckolding and then poisoning the Earl of Chester. It was one of the first stone castles in Britain. (For more on Castleton, see Walk 7.)

Walk southwest up Cave Dale, lined with limestone crags and stony underfoot, with the castle behind. Go through a swing-gate, pass some quarries and keep straight on towards Peak Forest. All around are the remains of old mineworkings. At Starvehouse Mine the route attains 1,542ft (471m). Eventually descend between two stone walls to a farm called The Cop **(2)**.

Turn right through the yard and head northwest down towards the wood at Oxlow Rake. Go left down the track and straight on over the wall-stile by Woodside Farm and Oxlow End. Walk half-left across the field after a yellow painted stile and keep on over wall-stiles, passing to the left of 'Smallwood' and through a small green gate.

Peveril Castle and Cave Dale

Just down the lane to the left are the hamlet of Old Dam and the village of Peak Forest, named after the medieval Royal Forest of the Peak. It grew up around the Chamber of the Peak (now Chamber Farm) which was built in the sixteenth century for the Peak Forest Ranger. It was there that the Swainmotes (forest courts) were held. The old church saw the weddings of many elopers in the eighteenth century, the incumbent being allowed to issue marriage licences. There is a shop in the village, and a pub, the Devonshire Arms.

Turn right up the track and walk northeast over the fields with good views back over the villages and past more mines. At a gate by two stiles towards the summit head east-northeast through the hummocks to find a stile in the corner of the fence by a large indentation in the ground. To the west is Eldon Hill with, on its south side, Eldon Hole, a chasm with a drop of 180ft (55m), one of the Seven Wonders of the Peak.

Head north-northeast towards the chimneys of Rowter Farm to find a gate giving on to a track (3). Turn left through the next gate and go over a ladder stile east towards Castleton, Mam Tor visible to the north. Now head back to the start, descending very steeply past the castle to the village.

Near Peak Forest

FACT FILE

Map OS Outdoor Leisure 1: The Dark Peak; Outdoor Leisure 24: The White Peak
Start/Finish SK 149830: Castleton car park. There are buses to Castleton from many places
Length 7 miles (11km)
Walking time 4 hours; allow longer if you wish to explore Peveril Castle
Difficulty A compass would be handy, otherwise easy enough

The Route in Brief

1 SK 149830. To Market Sq and Bargate and then up Cave Dale. Keep on Limestone Way to summit and eventually descend between 2 stone walls to The Cop farmhouse.
2 R through yard and NW to wood. L down track, straight on over stile, and

½L over more stiles to track by 'Smallwood'. R till gate by stiles. ENE through hummocks to stile in corner of fence by big indentation, then NNE towards chimneys of farm to track.
3 L through gate and over stile towards Castleton and back to start.

53

EYAM: THE PLAGUE VILLAGE

This walk is centred on the village of Eyam. It provides one stiff ascent through scrub and wood but is otherwise easy going. But to calculate this walk in terms of distance is irrelevant. There is so much to see in this unique place that anybody only slightly interested in the past should set aside the whole day to investigate it.

The extraordinary story of Eyam (pronounced 'Eem') brings visitors by the coach-load during the season. The village cannot escape its past, and largely because so many of the buildings that played a major part in it are still standing, it has become a monument to it. Despite this, and the fact that the tourist industry is obviously an important part of the local economy, Eyam retains a powerful and moving beauty and dignity, and the population go about their business much as any other Peak District community.

In the summer of 1665, the year of the Great Plague in London, a tailor named George Viccars, who was lodging in a cottage (still standing) near the church, received cloth he had ordered from London which may or may not have contained plague-carrying fleas. At any rate, Viccars shortly fell ill and died, being buried on 7 September. The son of his landlady succumbed to the same fever 15 days later, and several neighbours quickly followed him.

Panic now began to mount, and various families fled the village. The Rector, the Reverend William Mompesson, realised the seriousness of the consequences if the plague spread to the surrounding neighbourhood, and persuaded the villagers to quarantine themselves. From now on no one was to enter or leave the village. The villagers left money dipped in vinegar at various points around the village in exchange for provisions, particularly food, clothing and medical supplies, to be left by the outside world, largely by the arrangement of the Earl of Devonshire. This extraordinary collective act of bravery succeeded in stopping the spread of the disease. By October 1666, when the pestilence finally abated, 259 people from an estimated village population of 350 had perished.

The walk starts at the car park in Hawkhill Road (1). Turn left down into the village and then right. Pass Merril House, where Humphrey Merril died of the plague in September 1666. His brother Andrew had fled to a hut on Eyam Moor where he lived with his cockerel. One day, it is said, the bird took flight back to this house in Eyam. Andrew trusted its instinct and returned also to find that the danger of infection had abated. Pass also the birthplace of the local poet and author Richard Furness, born in 1791.

Take the next right (2) up a little lane through a farm and climb the stile, not easily seen at first, by the gate ahead. Now follow the wall north up the field. Note the tomb of Humphrey Merril at the bottom of the field to the right, sad and solitary. Follow the path that skirts left-handed round the garden of the house ahead and turns left up the track by the wall, continuing north uphill. Pass a mine spoil tip to the left and keep on fairly steeply through bracken and then northeasterly through a beech wood and across the tumbling Jumber Brook and on. Turn left up the track (3) and right at the lane. This is Occupation Road. There are now good views south over the village and quarry beyond. Ladywash Mine is to the north. Turn left at the end of the lane (4)

The Riley Graves, with the quarry at Stoney Middleton beyond

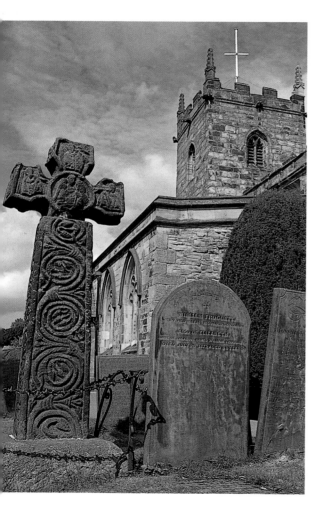

Eyam church with a Saxon cross

to visit Mompesson's Well. This was one of the plague boundaries established by Mompesson, where the outside world supplied provisions in exchange for coins left in the water-trough, to which vinegar had been added, by the villagers. There is a feeling of solemnity at this lonely spot, and it is not hard to imagine two or three villagers, haunted by fear of the disease, tramping up the road from the village to collect whatever had been left for them.

Retrace your steps to the junction of lanes, carrying straight on and taking the footpath on the left after the drive to Hollowbrook Barn. Descend south through the conifers of dark and gloomy Furness Wood, Hollow Brook to the right, to the village and turn left (5) at New Road. Fork left into the 'No Through Road' signposted to the Riley Graves, which are reached after a few minutes.

At a farm nearby the husband and six children of Elizabeth Hancock died within a week of each other in August 1666. Neighbours living across the valley to the south at Stoney Middleton are said to have watched the distraught woman drag out her dead and bury them in the graves she had dug. Amazingly she herself survived and escaped to Sheffield where she had a sole surviving son apprenticed in the cutlery trade. Her farmhouse lay abandoned for many years and was eventually pulled down. The central tomb

of her husband in the enclosure marks the only true grave. The rest of the headstones were transported here from their various original locations about the field.

Walk back into the village and turn left in the Square (6) up Lydgate. The Lydgate Graves, where George Darby, a lead miner, and his daughter Mary are buried, are soon seen on the right. Continue over the stile at the top of the lane and along the footpath southeast for about half a mile (1km) to visit the Boundary Stone. Money was placed in the holes, into which vinegar was first poured, in return for supplies.

Now retrace your steps back into the village where there are many other places of great interest to be investigated. Cucklet Church is a limestone grotto where the Rector held services rather than in church during the time of the plague. Obtain a key from the back door of Eyam Hall (for which a small charge is made) to the gate in the railings near the village stocks. Climb steeply down through the woods, cross the stream and climb again to the cavern over the shoulder of the rise ahead. There is a remarkable, still peace to be found here where William Mompesson intoned the prayers and blessings to a dwindling, grief-stricken and fearful congregation.

Eyam Hall was built shortly after the plague by Thomas Wright, and his descendants live in it still. Because very little was thrown away or changed over the years, it has a remarkable collection of furniture, ornaments, books, paintings, clothes and other objects long

A window in Eyam

associated with the house, and is very well worth a visit.

The little museum opposite the car park is both imaginative and rewarding, especially the splendid view of London in the plague year. The church of St Lawrence is full of interest, and its yard contains a fine Saxon Cross and the tomb of Katherine Mompesson, wife of the Rector. She had decided to stay in the village to support her husband. Perhaps the saddest memorial of all is the entry for the 200th casualty in the rector's register of plague deaths, written in his own hand: *1666. Aug. 25. Bur: Katharin ye wife of Mr. William Mompefson.*

FACT FILE

Map OS Outdoor Leisure 24: The White Peak
Start/Finish SK 216767: Eyam car park. Eyam can be reached by bus from several destinations
Length 3½ miles (5.5km)
Walking time 2 hours, but allow much longer if you want to visit the several interesting places in the village
Difficulty One reasonably steep climb

The Route in Brief

1 SK 216767. L into village, then R.
2 R through farm after Richard Furness's house. Ascend N through bracken, then NE through wood and over brook.
3 L at track and R at lane.
4 L at end of lane to visit well, then back S over junction and L down footpath leading S through wood to village.
5 L at New Road, then fork L (E) to Riley Graves and back to the village.
6 L in Square up Lydgate past Lydgate Grave to Boundary Stone and back.

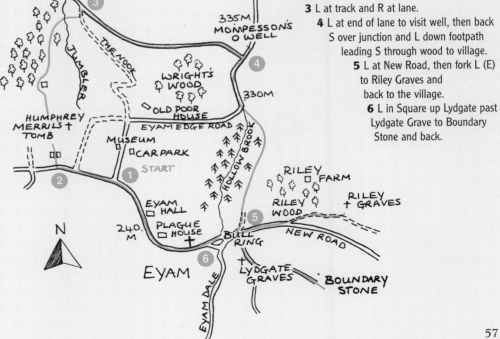

FIVE DALES

One of the finest dale walks of the White Peak, visiting five dales: Miller's, Water-cum-Jolly, Cressbrook, Tansley and Monk's. They range from picture-postcard pretty to dark and sombre, from flat and easy going to steep, rough and stony. You will encounter testing ascents, riverside strolling, and carefree striding 'over the tops'. Also two of the Derbyshire Dales' most attractive villages and reminders of the area's industrial heritage.

The walk begins at the car park at the western end of Miller's Dale. Turn left on to the Monsal Trail **(1)** and walk east. Far down below is the river Wye, following its beautiful course from the hill above Buxton to where it joins the Derwent at Rowsley. The Monsal Trail mostly follows the line of the disused St Pancras to Manchester railway opened in 1863 and felled 105 years later by

Left: The River Wye and the path through Miller's Dale
Far right: Cressbrook Mill

Beeching's axe. The building of the railway through the dales provoked the fury of John Ruskin, who would doubtless also have protested against the motor car which has caused so much more damage than the railway ever did. This stretch of the line is bordered by a wealth of wild flowers in summer – lady's bedstraw, scabious, willowherb, harebell, white campion and birdsfoot trefoil to mention a few – and on a hot day crickets chirp from the long grasses.

After about a mile and a half (2.5km) along the trail, and shortly after an overhead bridge, turn left **(2)**, signposted 'Water-cum-Jolly Dale'. Cross the footbridge and turn right through the gates of Litton Mill (there is a pub nearby). The first time I walked past these now-deserted buildings I found them sombre and oppressive. I was not surprised to find out subsequently that they have an unhappy history. First built in 1782, the mill soon became notorious for the treatment meted out by the owner, Ellis Needham, to his workforce, which then included young children from impoverished families. A certain feeling of unhappiness lingers.

Go right at the end of the buildings and left on to the riverbank. Now things improve dramatically. The Wye is a lovely, clean and healthy river, teeming with wildlife. In a short summer stroll you could encounter ducks, water-voles, coots, moorhen and trout rising to take the fly. The river bends round into Water-cum-Jolly Dale. Limestone cliffs rise on each

side, and bullrushes grow from the still waters. Cross the footbridge at the end (you have come about a mile and a half (2.5km) from Litton Mill) and turn left through the stoneyard. You will now see Cressbrook Mill, derelict but handsome, and altogether more pleasing than Litton. This was built in 1815 on the site of one of Arkwright's mills and was for a time managed by William Newton, the 'Minstrel of the Peak'. By all accounts the workers and apprentices here were treated well, housed comfortably and even given a little schooling. Note the bellcote on top of the building for summoning them to work.

Turn left at the road **(3)** and ascend north for 600 yards/metres (ignoring the steep road immediately on your left). Turn right down a small lane signposted 'Ravensdale' through a mixed wood of tall trees. Keep on past some cottages. The cliffs to the east across the valley were indeed frequented by ravens, while Ravencliffe Cave was much inhabited by man from the Neolithic Age on. The trees beneath are a fine and rare example of natural ash woodland.

Follow the path through the wood and across a footbridge into Cressbrookdale. Now climb steeply northeast up the east side of the valley, eventually meeting a stile at the top. You will be feeling satisfied enough with the day's work, but a glance at the terrain will show you that there is a great deal more to do.

Do not climb the stile. Instead, turn left **(4)** and descend northwest back into the valley. At

the bottom cross a stile and climb west up Tansley Dale. Swing right up a wall at the top of the dale **(5)**, cross a stile, go half-right to the next stile in the field corner, turn left into the old stony lane, and right over the first stile, keeping northwest all the time into Litton **(6)**. It is an attractive village, standing at about 1000ft. Turn left (west) through the village, past a shop on the left, and then fork right past the Red Lion pub, famous for its traditional music nights, opposite which stand the village stocks. Pass the church and walk along the lane, dropping down into Tideswell.

Tideswell (nicknamed Tidzer) is a charming place, uncertain whether it is a large village or a small town. There are many shops, pubs and facilities for walkers. The superb church of St John the Baptist is known as the 'Cathedral of the Peak'. It was built over about 50 years in the fourteenth century, interrupted by the Black Death, and has few rivals in Derbyshire.

Turn left through Tideswell **(7)**. There are several other notable buildings to look at, including Markeygate House on the corner. Towards the end of the village, at the Horse and Jockey pub, fork right up Queen Street and immediately right again up an alley, Primrose Lane, across the road and over a stile. Now there is a very pleasing western ascent over ten fields by stiles **(8)**, crossing a lane, to a green lane. Cross this and walk up

Drystone walls between Tideswell and Monk's Dale

the centre of the next two fields to another lane, part of the Limestone Way. Turn right, down to the house, and then left down the lane. At the bottom leave the Limestone Way, instead turning left (south) down Monk's Dale (9). This steep-sided nature reserve is quiet, secluded, at times dark and eerie, and the rough rocky path makes for hard going. In wet weather conditions can be treacherous. There was once a grange and chapel in the dale, hence its name, and legend has it that there is a tunnel leading to Tideswell church. After about a mile and a half (2.5km), leave Monk's Dale by a gate leading down to the road. Turn right under the viaduct, then right again back to the car park.

Map OS Outdoor Leisure 24: The White Peak
Start/Finish SK 137733: car park at Miller's Dale old station. Miller's Dale is well served by bus routes
Length 10 miles (16km)
Walking time 5 hours (more if you wish to explore Tideswell)
Difficulty Generally easy going with one steep ascent. The last stretch, down Monk's Dale, is hard going underfoot

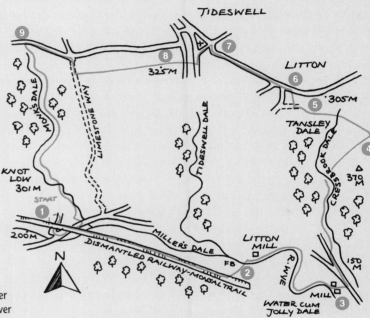

The Route in Brief

1 SK 137733. From car park turn L along Monsal Trail and walk E for 1½ miles (2.5km).
2 After overhead bridge turn L, signed 'Water-cum-Jolly Dale', over river, past Litton Mill and along river for 1½ miles (2.5km).
3 L at road and keep R (N) uphill, taking small road on R signed 'Ravensdale', past cottages, over footbridge and steeply, N then NE, up Cressbrookdale.
4 At stile at top turn L (NW) down into dale, over stile and L (W) up Tansley Dale.
5 Swing R up wall and take stiles over fields and a lane NW to Litton.
6 L in village. Fork R past pub and NW along lane to Tideswell.

7 L in village, R up Queen St by Horse and Jockey pub, R up valley, across road and over stile.
8 Ascend W, crossing 10 fields and a lane, to a green lane. Walk up next two fields, turn R at lane and L at next lane.
9 Turn L down Monk's Dale and walk S for 1½ miles (2.5km). Leave by gate down to road, R under viaduct and R back to start.

61

LONGSTONE MOOR

The two villages of Little and Great Longstone are both visited on this fairly short and easy route which climbs above both along an ancient track and crosses a satisfying stretch of open moorland with excellent views before returning by woods, lane, scrub and pastureland.

Facing the Packhorse pub **(1)** (highly recommended), take the path opposite to its left signed 'Cherpit Lane for Wardlow'. Follow stiles, crossing the first two large fields diagonally and keeping on north up a smartly kept wall. Turn right on to a lovely old track, Cherpit Lane, and head east, with fine views to the southeast towards Chatsworth and Haddon. Turn left over stiles at the picnic area. Continue past a track coming in from the right and climb a stile over a wall **(2)**. More excellent views have now opened up ahead.

Turn right up the wall, continue for a short distance where it turns right, and turn right

A frozen dewpond below Longstone Edge, Monsal Dale in the distance

through a gateway, ascending the obvious path through patches of heather on to Longstone Moor. Pass a tumulus on the left and follow the line of sycamores ahead to pick up a path leading east-southeast along a broken wall and across the rake of a mine. A hundred and twenty yards/metres after a solitary stone gatepost turn right along a path leading south between a single and a pair of Scots pines. Great Longstone comes into sight below.

Cross a stile and follow the path curling down through the wood. Turn left up a lane (3) for some time. As it bends sharply left, cross a stile and slant right-handed down the bank, picking up a path which cuts southwest through the scrub and leads down to a stile. Cross a field and skirt right-handed round a rocky bank, taking the broad green swathe leading down the little valley. Before the end fork right by a footpath sign up along the bank and follow stiles, a path and a track south into Great Longstone (4). (For Great and Little Longstone see Walk 19.) Turn right into the village and bend to the left by the churchyard. Turn right past the White Lion and left towards Thornbridge Hall (the Griffin pub is just beyond this turn). Towards the end of the village turn right at a stile in the wall by a footpath sign and head west back to Little Longstone across the fields. When you reach the pub you can continue past it west along the lane to the junction, where there are famous views over Monsal Dale and the valley of the Wye.

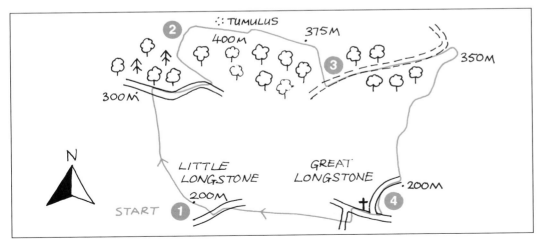

FACT FILE

Map OS Outdoor Leisure 24: The White Peak
Start/Finish SK 191717: Little Longstone. There are buses to Little Longstone
Length 5 miles (8km)
Walking time 2½ hours
Difficulty Easy walking

The Route in Brief

1 SK 191717. Up path by pub signed 'Cherpit Lane' and over stiles N to track. R to picnic site, where L over stiles, past track coming in, to stile over wall.
2 R up wall and R through gateway. Pass tumulus, follow line of sycamores and then path along broken wall. Cross mine-rake; 120 yards/metres past stone gatepost turn R along path to stile and down through wood.
3 L up lane and over stile at sharp L bend. Down bank to find path leading SW through scrub to stile. Path leads to rocky bank then broad swathe. R at footpath sign over stiles to Great Longstone.
4 R into village, L by churchyard, R past pub and L towards Thornbridge Hall. R at stile near end of village and W to Little Longstone.

THE MIDDLE OF THE PEAK

Left: The weir on the Wye
Opposite: Bretton Edge from Taddington

Monsal Dale is famously beautiful, and this route ends with a gentle amble along the banks of the Wye. But before that it explores the higher ground around Taddington, making very satisfactory use of some ancient tracks and lanes, and at about halfway climbs to a viewpoint which is central to the Peak District, allowing a vast area of it to be surveyed.

Climb the steps leading out of the car park (1) and head south over stiles, ignoring a path to the right. The route rounds an outcrop of rocks and takes the obvious path signed 'Deepdale', swinging round to meet a path coming in from the right and following the wall up. Deepdale is a dry limestone dale with steep, partially wooded side. The southwest wind has a habit of funnelling down it, making progress difficult. As the dale shallows and widens the path crosses to the other side of the wall and, towards the top, meets a track coming across (2).

Turn right here and walk north. Behind to the southeast Magpie Mine (see Walk 19) is gauntly outlined against the rising ground. Longstone Edge juts up to the northeast over Monsal Dale. Pass Over Wheal Farm, old mines to the left, and at a crossways take a track to the left which heads northwest between disused mines and with a superb series of walls to the right. Flagg village lies to the south.

Go right at the road, with views north to Brown Knoll and Kinder Scout, and northeast to the radio mast on Sir William Hill above Eyam and to Bretton Edge, where it is possible to make out the white-painted Barrell Inn. To the left of that is Hucklow Edge. Shortly turn right down a green lane towards Taddington (pub and shop), one of the highest villages in England at about 1,000ft (305m), going left through a stile by a gate just before the edge of the village. Cross a patch of common ground west to a gate giving on to a lane leading to a road. Turn right and then left up a path at Daybreak Cottage just before a junction.

Now climb the fields, crossing a lane, with flat-topped Fin Cop to the east, and, at Sough Top (1,437ft/438m) **(3)**, be rewarded with one of the finest views in the Peak District, first shown to me by Mike Williams. Its particular joy is that, being almost central, it extends over the Dark and White Peak, from north to south and far into the east. To the north is the rare sight of the whole of the Kinder plateau, with Lose Hill to its right. Tideswell is straight ahead, with Litton on its right, and to the east

can be seen the hunting tower above Chatsworth, the Eastern Edges jutting into the skyline above it. To the south there is also a magnificent sweep, including Minninglow Hill, distinguished by its few stunted trees on top, and Hazelton Clump above Ashbourne at the end of the high country.

Go right along the wall after the little reservoir and continue west, Moor Grange behind the trees to the left and the moors above Buxton on the western skyline. Turn right at the broad green lane – part of the Limestone Way – and head north. To the west, on private land, are the upright stones of the Neolithic Five Wells Burial Chamber. Descend to the Waterloo Inn and cross the A6 **(4)**.

Walk straight on down the lane ahead and over the crossroads into Priestcliffe, a charming backwater hamlet, with some pronounced strip lynchets to the right. At Lydgate Farm follow the sign to Monsal Dale. This excellent track provides some lovely, easy walking. It bends right at New Barn, past mines to right and left, and turns southeast after a nature reserve, descending with High Dale on the right past Top and Middle Farms and turning left, again signed 'Monsal Dale', through Lower. Be considerate here: the route is open to motor traffic and the farmers must get quite fed up with the world going by their windows.

Now head east, with Taddington Dale to the right and with beautiful views up the valley of the Wye, the A6 mercifully concealed. Keep on at the sign 'Monsal Dale and Trail', with Fin

Above The viaduct over Monsal Dale
Left: The Wye in Monsal Dale

Cop to the right. The fort or settlement on its top is thought to date from the first century BC and enclosed an area of about ten acres. Down in the dale can be seen a weir and the rocks of Hob's House. At the bend leading north down to a road head straight on, signed 'Public Bridleway', along an often extremely muddy stretch. Ahead is the railway viaduct about which John Ruskin fumed:

You enterprised a railroad through the valley – you blasted its rocks away, heaped thousands of tons of shale into its lovely stream. The valley is gone and the Gods with it, and now

every fool in Buxton can be at Bakewell in half an hour and every fool in Bakewell at Buxton; which you think a lucrative process of exchange – you Fools everywhere.

Well, it's not as bad as all that. The viaduct, unlovely though it is, might now be considered a bonus, providing as it does a splendid view of Monsal Dale. But one takes Ruskin's point, perhaps in a modern age transferring his odium for the railways to the roads.

You have now only to turn right along the river (5) (take the path on the other side if you still have energy to expend) to return past the weir down the 'divine' valley to the car park, taking care not to be mown down on the A6 by one of the Bakewell 'fools' hastening to be at Buxton in ten minutes flat.

Map OS Outdoor Leisure 24: The White Peak
Start/Finish SK 171705: White Lodge car park on A6 at southern end of Monsal Dale
Length 10½ miles (17km)
Walking time 5 hours
Difficulty A couple of long climbs, otherwise easy

The Route in Brief

1 SK 171705. Up steps and S, ignoring path to R. Round rocks towards Deepdale, meeting path coming in from R and following wall all the way up dale to track.

2 R past farm and L at crossways along track. R at road and R down green lane. L over stile just before village, W across common ground to gate on to lane. R at road and L at path before junction. Up fields, crossing lane, to summit.

3 R along wall after reservoir and W till R at green lane (Limestone Way) down to road.

4 Cross A6 to lane ahead and over crossroads to Priestcliffe. Take track to Monsal Dale, following signs.

5 R at viaduct down Monsal Dale back to start.

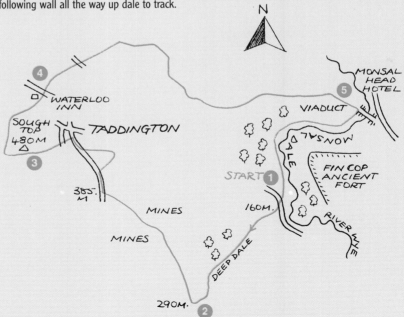

FIVE VILLAGES AND BAKEWELL

This lengthy and absorbing walk begins and ends at Bakewell and explores a good deal of the country to its east, remaining for much of its time 'on the tops', but dipping down to cross the Wye at Ashford and visiting four other villages. It includes a detour to Magpie Mine, a fascinating monument to the days of lead mining.

Bakewell is sometimes known as the 'capital of the Peak' and has paid a high price for its popularity in recent years, becoming uncomfortably crowded in summer. One cannot help but question the wisdom of policies such as the Derbyshire Dales District Council's constant promotion of tourism. Isn't it time to call a halt? There is much of interest to be seen in the town, not least in the church of All Saints (1) with its elegant spire, superb monuments and huge collection of ancient gravestones and covers,

and on Mondays there is an excellent market.

From South Church Street, which becomes Monyash Road, walk uphill. Turn left into Yeld Road and right at The Yeld. Follow the path southwest through a new housing estate, across the playing fields of Lady Manners School, across the road, and on, turning south uphill to the road. Turn left up it, round the bend and past the drive to Burton Manor Farm. Take the stile on the left, making use of the 'nick' which dips down and up to meet the road again, having cut off the corner. Turn left down the road into Over Haddon. This is a thriving little village overlooking the glories of Lathkill Dale. There is a post office, a tea-room or two and an excellent inn, the Lathkill Hotel.

Go right (2) towards Monyash, turning right over the stile at the end of the village. Now climb north then northwest over fields and the B5055 and on over more fields before eventually descending, Magpie Mine now in view to the west, to the road at Kirk

South towards Kirk Dale

Left: Magpie Mine

Dale. Walk west up the walled green lane opposite to visit the mine (**3**).

Lead was mined here from the seventeenth century until 1958, sometimes successfully and at others disastrously. It is the best-preserved lead mine in the country and stands as a sombre monument to the thousands of Derbyshire men who toiled in dreadful and dangerous conditions over the centuries to extract the heaviest, softest and weakest of the common metals. There is a certain mournfulness here.

Leave the mine on the footpath heading north, signed 'Ashford' to Sheldon village, which has no pub or shop. Turn right at the road and left down the path just after the farmhouse on the bend. Descend northeast through Little Shacklow Wood and turn right along the Wye. This stretch is likely to be boggy and slippery. Go left at the lane to the main road (**4**) and turn right and shortly left over the bridge into Ashford in the Water. It is a pretty village with shops and a good pub, the Bull's Head. Medieval Sheepwash Bridge just downstream is a particularly fine example of its type. It was across this that hundreds of packhorses would pass in the old days, the village lying on the ancient Portway track.

Walk straight through the village, north, and fork right up Vicarage Lane. Ascend past Highfield Farm and take the stile on the right across the field to a road. Cross it and then a lane, continuing northerly past lovely trees, and finally a disused railway line before gaining the road at Little Longstone (turn left to the Packhorse, one of Derbyshire's best pubs). Little Longstone Manor is the home of the Longsdon family, who have lived in the village for seven centuries.

Turn right at the stile without leaving the field, east, at an acute angle to the path you have just been on, towards Great Longstone (**5**). The present Hall is eighteenth century and, unusually for the Peak, is built of brick. The Wright family lived here for many hundreds of years until the 1920s. There are two pubs. Turn right at the road along the edge of the village and go straight on through the gate at the bend in the road. Turn left (east) along the disused railway, the Monsal Trail, and cross a road and then the main road. Turn right at the end of the wood which lies on the right (**6**).

Climb up the track and then make the pleasant descent on the old road to Bakewell, Stanton Moor ahead to the south-southeast. Turn left at the road opposite the packhorse bridge and right at the stile over the meadows to the river, taking the right of two stiles leading to Scott's Meadows along the river. Turn right at the bridge back into Bakewell.

Right: The Wye at Ashford

Map OS Outdoor Leisure 24: The White Peak
Start/Finish SK 215685: South Church Street, Bakewell. Bakewell is well served by buses
Length 11 miles (17.5km)
Walking time 5 hours. Allow extra for time spent at Magpie Mine and exploring Bakewell and the villages
Difficulty Easy walking

The Route in Brief

1 SK 215685. From South Church St walk uphill. L into Yeld Rd, R at The Yeld, and SW through housing estate, across playing fields and road, and S to road. L round bend, L down and up 'nick', L at road and R towards Monyash.

2 R over stile at end of village then NW up over fields, B5055 and down to road at Kirk Dale. Up green lane W to Magpie Mine.

3 N, signed 'Ashford', to Sheldon. R at road, L down path after house, through woods. R along river and L at lane to road.

4 R and L over bridge. Straight on through Ashford, R up Vicarage Lane, R across field after Highfield Farm. Cross road and N over lane and old railway to Little Longstone. Double back in V shape E to Great Longstone.

5 R at road, straight on through gate at bend and E along Monsal Trail over 2 roads and R at end of wood on R.

6 Up and down track, L opposite bridge, R at stile to river, R of 2 stiles, along river, and R at bridge back to start.

72

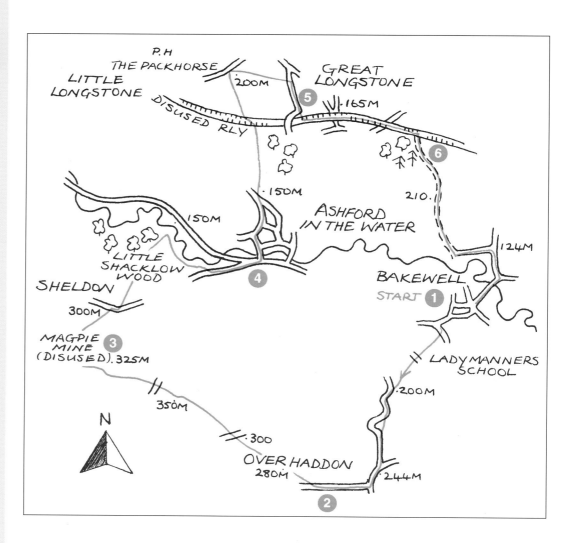

TAXAL EDGE AND THE GOYT VALLEY

This route rises to cross Taxal Moor and Edge and explore the fine piece of country west of Goyt Forest, a patchwork of brooks, valleys, farmsteads and hills, before returning over the tops and heading back north along the River Goyt, celebrated for its beauty and peacefulness.

From the car park (1) walk down the track to the river, crossing at the footbridge and ascending to the lane by Taxal church, which contains a memorial tablet to Michael Heathcote, 'Gentleman of the Pantry and Yeoman of the Mouth' to George II. For many centuries Taxal was part of the estates of the Jodrell family, whose name is now best remembered by Jodrell Bank. There is a pub to the right.

Turn left then right up the footpath signed 'Taxal Edge' opposite Glebe Farm, leading west straight ahead up a wall. Cross the lane and keep on up through the conifers, then climb steeply through heather and rhododendrons. Hawks may be gliding above. If you lose the track, head slightly to the right, marginally north of due west, towards a gap in the top wall to the right of five small oaks, a tree stump and a post, where you will find a stile. This is Taxal Edge (2), the boundary between Derbyshire and Cheshire, with marvellous views back northeast to the great mass of Kinder Scout.

Descend westerly to the lane. To the north the hills rise above Todd Brook, culminating in Whaley Moor and Black Hill. Turn right and take the path to the left. Now head half-left, walking south across the field to a stile. The craggy outline of the aptly named Windgather Rocks now appears cresting Taxal Edge to the south. Keeping south, pass through the gate in the opposite corner of the field and continue, keeping the wall on your right, down to Wright's Farm (3).

Walk through the yard, passing to the left of the buildings, and cross the stile by the vegetable patch. Head left to a bend in the wall, then pick up the path leading to the right, by-passing Clough Farm. Descend westerly over the brook and past two farms. At the second farm, after the track bends to the right towards Kettleshulme, take the stile on the left, continuing west to a lane (4).

Cross and take the track curving south. Pass, perhaps muddily at times, through Thorneycroft, Neighbourway and Near Carr Farms. Go through the gate after the next house and turn right, through the gate ahead where the hedges meet, down the hedge and along the track, west, over the footbridge at Todd Brook and steeply uphill the other side. The Windgather Rocks to the east across the valley have now assumed a very different shape.

Cross the stile up to Charles Head Farm (5) and turn left through the buildings. Walk south along the path past a barn and over a stile, with fine views ahead, and fork half-left down the brackeny hillside to find a stile to a path leading south across two brooks and descending to Summer Close Farm. Keep to the left of the buildings and take the track which climbs southwards along the line of a wall and along the side of Cook Hill (6). You are now above 1,200ft (365m).

Turn left along the lane and walk east down towards Jenkin Chapel. This early eighteenth-century building was built on the route of the old saltway from Northwich to Chesterfield. There is a house due south called Saltersford Hall. Fork left at the junction for a few yards and take the path to the left leading northeast to Green Stack Farm. Cross the stile at the end of the buildings and head north up the wall. Cross a brook and continue north past a barn.

Keep just left of the rough grass and follow a fenced wall to a stile.

Follow this path through the garden of Dunge Farm (7) (where teas are available in summer) and on north along the track which becomes a lane leading up to a road, Windgather Rocks to the right. Cross the road and fork right up a track to Black Hill Gate Farm which sits on the county border on Taxal Edge, and on up to the summit at about 1,250ft (380m), meeting heather, bilberries and splendid views again. Descend east, taking the lane down to Overton Hall Farm (8). There has been a house of importance here since the thirteenth century at least, the most recent version of which, associated with the Jodrells, was demolished in the early nineteenth century.

Continue down the track, round the hairpin to the right. Cross Mill Clough and turn hard left. Climb up the track past beautifully kept Knipe Farm, continuing down to the dam at Fernilee Reservoir. Cross it and head north down the River Goyt back to the start in the car park.

Above: Fernilee Reservoir
Opposite: Northwards to the Kinder Plateau from Overton Hall Farm

Map OS Outdoor Leisure 24: The White Peak
Start/Finish SK 008799: car park off A5004 south of Whaley Bridge and just east of Taxal. There is a station at Whaley Bridge
Length 9.75 miles (15.5km)
Walking time 5 hours
Difficulty A couple of steep climbs. A compass would be helpful

The Route in Brief

1 SK 008799. Down track and across river to lane. L then R up path signed 'Taxal Edge'.

2 Descend W to lane. R and L down path leading S to Wright's Farm.

3 Through farm, over stile, L to bend in wall and take path leading W. At 2nd farm take stile on L as track bends R. Path leads to lane.

4 Cross and take track S through 3 farms. R after next house, down to footbridge over brook and up to Charles Head Farm.

5 L and S to Summer Close Farm. Take track S to Cook Hill.

6 L down lane to Jenkin Chapel. Fork L then take path on L (NE) to Green Stack Farm, then N up wall, across brook, past barn, L of rough grass, and along fenced wall to Dunge Farm.

7 N along track becoming lane to road. Cross road and fork R up track past farm to summit. Down E to Overton Hall Farm.

8 Down to Mill Clough and hard L up past Knipe Farm, down across dam and N up river back to start.

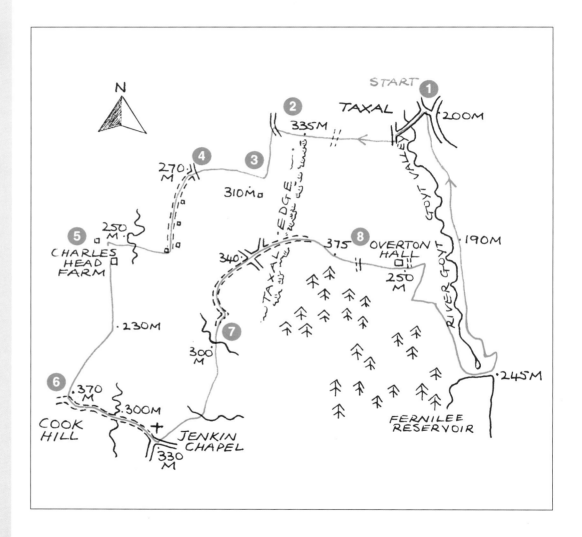

COMBS EDGE

While most walkers and nearly all tourists choose to explore the Goyt valley just to the west, the area to the south of Combs village offers splendid opportunities for a day's tramp. Combs Edge dramatically rises to the east, an ancient fort sitting aloft, with bleak Combs Moss rising beyond to Black Edge at 1,663ft (507m). The walk explores the fort and the farmland below.

From Chapel-en-le-Frith railway station (1) cross the railway line and fork right down the drive of Bank Hall Lodge, passing it and keeping on up through the beech trees. Combs Reservoir can be seen to the right, and the fort at Castle Naze comes into view to the left. Continue past the next lodge, then Bank Hall. Pass through Bank Hall Farm, the fort now looming above ahead. Climb to the road and take the path up to the fort.

This is a thrilling place, probably first fortified by Iron Age Man and kept in use by the Romans and their successors. It sits almost impregnably at about 1,550ft (470m) at the northern tip of Combs Edge, with Short Edge striking out behind it to the east and the Moss rising to Hob Tor, and commands superb views.

Retrace your steps to the lane and turn left, descending steeply round the bend and passing the entrances to Pyegreave Farm and Moss View, with brooks on both sides of the road. Go left immediately after the entrance to Rye Flatt (2), walking past Rye Flatt Farm and Bracken Clough and south along the track towards Allstone Lee Farm. At the bend after the bungalow keep straight on over stile and footbridge signed 'White Hall'. Descend muddily to two footbridges, forking left after the second to climb to a stile in the wall. Follow the wall up southwest and cross the pasture to Combshead Farm, passing to the right of the buildings. Cross the track. The path then climbs relentlessly, parallel to the brook and following the walls.

Turn right down the track by the White Hall Centre (for outdoor pursuits) (3) and swing right, round the bend, heading north, following the course of a Roman road. Fork right at the junction and turn left down the

View from Castle Naze

track to Hazelhurst Farm. Follow the footpath leading round the buildings (not the one off to the right) and keep on north, diagonally across the field and skirting the hawthorns, to Haylee Farm, Combs Edge now running parallel to the east. Do not take the path to the left, but walk through the yard and round the cowshed, following the length of the building, and on north-northwest, down over the brook and up to Thorney Lee (4). To the north, over Ladder Hill, is Tunstead Farm where the legend of the haunted skull of 'Dickey o' Tunstead' persisted for several centuries.

Skirt the barn and turn right through the yard, heading east down the wall of the pasture through a stile to a track. Turn right at the lane into Combs village past the Beehive Inn, bearing right out of the village towards Dove Holes. Take the footpath to the left after the entrance to Rye Flatt, signed 'Chapel-en-le-Frith Station'. Now climb steeply northeast, slanting away from the brook and keeping to the left of the wall ahead. Keep up the middle of the next two fields and so along the hillside, the railway below, and back to the station, where there is a good restaurant.

Combs Edge, Castle Naze to the left

Map OS Outdoor Leisure 24: The White Peak
Start/Finish SK 054796: Chapel-en-le-Frith station
Length 6½ miles (10.5km)
Walking time 4 hours
Difficulty A couple of fairly steep climbs

The Route in Brief

1 SK 054796. Cross line, R past Bank Hall and lodge, and through farm to road. Detour to fort. Then L (W) at lane.
2 L after entrance to Rye Flatt and S along track. Take path for White Hall, forking L after 2nd bridge and ascending past Combshead Farm.
3 R past White Hall, R round bend, R at junction and L to Hazelhurst Farm. N to Haylee Farm and on NNW up to Thorney Lee.
4 E into Combs, R out of village, L for 'Chapel-en-le-Frith Station'.

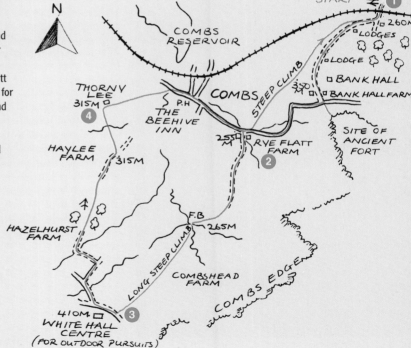

THE CAT AND FIDDLE

The Cat and Fiddle Inn

This wild and lonely route begins and ends at this famous inn and remains entirely on high moorland, switching between Cheshire, Derbyshire and Staffordshire. It descends to the River Goyt, climbs over Goyt's Moss and Axe Edge Moor and swings back round by the huge and eerie abandoned quarry of Danebower.

At 1,690ft (515m) above sea level, the Cat and Fiddle pub is the second highest in England, outranked only by the Tan Hill Tavern in North Yorkshire, some 42ft (13m) higher. Its view is famous, stretching west to the Mersey and the Welsh hills. Facing the pub (1), walk down the road to the left and take the track to the right at the first bend. This is part of the original turnpike from Macclesfield to Buxton, known as the Stonyway, which was built in 1759. Its surface is much as it was then, and it is not hard to conjure up images of the horses, carts and coaches rumbling and crunching over this desolate moor without even the prospect of the inn, built later, to cheer them on.

The old road forks off to the left ahead, but follow the track round to the right as it runs along the border between Cheshire and Derbyshire. Turn east into the latter at a sign to Goyt's Clough. Come to woodland on the left and cross Stake Clough and then a track, and continue round the edge of the plantation. A stile leads to a path through the trees. Cross Deep Clough and keep on northeast through the wood. At a stile at its end fork right along its edge and descend to a lane.

Turn left and soon descend to a footbridge across the newly risen River Goyt (2). We have descended some 550ft (165m) from the pub but now start to climb again, heading east up the stream and eventually crossing another coming in from the east. Look back west to see the Cat and Fiddle on the skyline, where it remains to taunt us for much of the route. Fork right by a cairn and post, and swing round to the south. Turn left along a wall at a stile, Buxton visible ahead, and shortly turn right. Fork right just after a brook, climb the stile by a gate, go right along the path for a few steps and cross the main road to a gate just after the bend (3).

This is Axe Edge Moor, named after the gritstone edge to the south. The annual rainfall is some 50in (1,250mm), and three of the Peak's main rivers, the Goyt, the Dane and the Dove have their sources here. Keep south past the hummocks of Thatch Marsh and turn right at the road and then left towards Three Shires Head. Cross the infant Dane River, whose source is just north of the road, then a stile in a wall into Staffordshire. Now walk straight ahead (south) between and away from the converging walls, the county boundary, down and along the ravine, soon meeting a track heading south-southwest. Shortly after the track straightens out, cut across the coarse grass south-southwest to the tumbledown buildings of unkempt Orchard Farm, climbing a stile in the wall. Pass through the yard, passing directly to the left of the farmhouse, scale the gate and cross the field ahead. This farm and its neighbour must feel even more remote than they are because of the very difficult access to them.

Turn right up the track (4) and head straight on, crossing a fence and continuing northerly round the side of the hill. If you happen to be walking on a hot summer's day, let me assure you that this stretch of the walk in winter with a cold north wind is strength-sapping. Pass through the abandoned quarries of Reeve-edge and Danebower, sad and eerie whatever the weather, crossing the Dane again back into Cheshire. Turn steeply right up the bank by the chimney and cross the road to the old track leading northwest and then north back to the Cat and Fiddle.

FACT FILE

Map OS Outdoor Leisure 24: The White Peak
Start/Finish SK 001719: the Cat and Fiddle public house on the A537 Macclesfield road from Buxton. It can be reached by bus
Length 9 miles (14.5km)
Walking time 5 hours
Difficulty A compass would be helpful

The Route in Brief

1 SK 001719. Facing pub, L down road, R at bend, round to R, R towards Goyt's Clough, through wood, L at road and cross river.
2 E up clough, crossing another. R at cairn and post, L and R over stiles, R after brook, over stile, R for a few steps and cross road to gate after bend.

3 S along path past hummocks. R at road and L towards Three Shires Head. Across stream and stile and straight ahead down ravine. After track straightens cut across SSW to farm. Pass to L of house, and over gate and field.
4 R up track, cross fence and round hill. Through quarry and across stream. R up steep bank by chimney. Cross road to track leading NW and N back to pub.

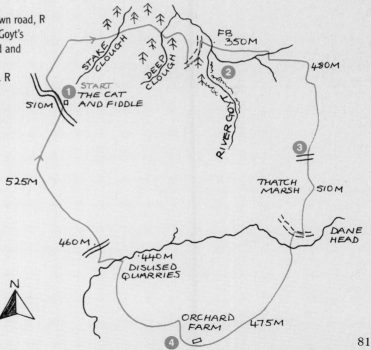

81

MACCLESFIELD FOREST AND SHUTLINGSLOE HILL

This walk on the western fringe of the Peak District is entirely in Cheshire. It begins among the conifers of Macclesfield Forest, then crosses farmland and moor to the tiny hamlet of Wildboarclough, and finally climbs to the summit of Shutlingsloe Hill, from where there are stupendous views across the plain of Cheshire.

The Forest of Macclesfield was once far larger than the plantation of conifers that remains. From the car park **(1)**, turn left on to the road and left again at the junction signed 'Higher Sutton and Wincle'. At a bend to the left carry straight on over the stile by a gate, signed 'Langley via Gritstone Trail'. This path leads through the wood to Ridgegate Reservoir. Turn left, then left again away from the reservoir signed 'Forest Walk'. Turn left at a stile signed 'Gritstone Trail' (noting Jodrell Bank Radio Telescope in the distant west) and cross the stream at the footbridge.

Turn left (south) along the Gritstone Trail.

At the road **(2)** go straight over, up the steps in the opposite bank. Look back to see Tegg's Nose to the west of the forest as you climb up from the valley bottom. At the road turn left towards Wincle, leaving the Trail. Take the second footpath to the right and climb some steps. Note the radar mast to the southwest and the Welsh hills in the far distance.

Cross the road at the Hanging Gate free house and take the path signed 'Greenway Bridge'. Macclesfield is now spread out behind to the northwest. Cross the stile at the edge of High Moor, walking through gorse and rough grass, and turn right through the gateway.

Turn left up the path towards Shutlingsloe Hill in the distance and walk east-southeast. Pass a pond **(3)** and fork right. Cross a stile over the wall in front of the houses at Oakenclough to the next stile, down through the gate and so southeast down the valley, crossing the Oaken Clough stream, then following it.

Turn left up the road and shortly fork left up the lane, the valley of the Highmoor Brook to the right. Where the lane bends sharply to the left **(4)**, cross a stile ahead and turn left over a stile by a gate. Walk half-right in an easterly direction down the pastures over a series of stiles. The tip of Shutlingsloe Hill appears again to the north. Continue down the road to the Crag Inn (free house). Turn left here and shortly left again at the bend up the private road. Follow the path up Shutlingsloe Hill, leaving Crag Hall and the hamlet of Wildboarclough behind and below to the southeast. It was once a busy little place, the territory of the earls of Derby and the site of silk mills powered by Clough Brook until the competition of steam was to cause their abandonment. Only one part of the old buildings, Crag Mill, remains.

One path now leads round the hill, and one to the top **(5)**. It is certainly worth taking the latter. The views are breathtaking from the 1,659ft (506m) summit. On a clear day Kinder Scout is just visible tucked in behind the bulk of Shining Tor (1,834ft/559m) to the north. To the west the Clwydian Hills in Wales may be plainly seen. To the southwest are the

Shutlingsloe from Oakenclough

Map OS Outdoor Leisure 24: The White Peak
Start/Finish SK 962712: car park off road at southwest corner of Trentabank Reservoir
Length 7¼ miles (11.5km)
Walking time 4 hours
Difficulty A stiff climb towards the end, otherwise easy enough

The Route in Brief

1 SK 962712. L on to road, L at junction, straight on at bend, L at reservoir, L signed 'Forest Walk', then follow Gritstone Trail signs.

2 Straight over road up steps, L at road, R at 2nd footpath up steps, over road at pub towards Greenway Bridge, over stile, R through gateway, and L up path towards hill.

3 Pass pond and fork R. Cross stiles by houses and descend valley, crossing stream, L at road and fork L up lane.

4 Cross stile at bend in lane and L at next stile. Descend pastures E to pub at road. L then L at private road. Ascend to summit of hill.

5 Descend N, then NW along paved track back to forest. Track to L, then L towards Trentabank. Straight on till L at road.

Cloud and Mow Cop, and to the southeast the Roaches and Ramshaw Rocks. As we walked over Shutlingsloe for this book, the afternoon pulled out a full bag of tricks. A fitful storm began to lash the Cheshire plain with scattered bursts of rain, while yellowing clouds stood out before a dark grey backdrop in a manner only Turner could have done justice to.

The path descends from the hill in a northerly direction to a stile. (If you have rounded the hill, head east-northeast from the stile, ignoring the sign which points to Langley straight ahead, to another). Now a stone-flagged path leads northwest back to the forest, at the entry to which another track leads leftwards. Take it and turn left towards Trentabank, keep straight on at the next signposts and turn left at the road back to the car park.

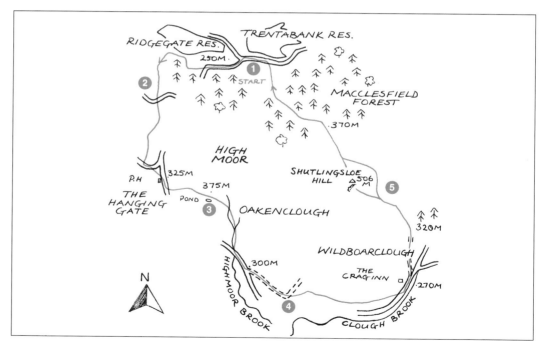

HOLLINSCLOUGH

The hills and dales around Hollinsclough, south of the quarries of Buxton, offer plenty of fine walking. This route investigates much of the best of that country, twice crossing the Staffordshire/Derbyshire border, and revelling in some typical White Peak farmland and scenery.

Set off up the attractive village **(1)** past the chapel on the right. This was built in 1801 for £355 by John Lomas, a successful jaggerman. He was a convert to and preacher of Methodism, and lies buried here in a vault. The dramatic, sheer, limestone reef knolls of Chrome Hill are on the right, with Parkhouse Hill further back to the east. Continue past a farm on the right to a bridleway post. Follow the path downhill with Hollins Hill ahead. This is the first in a distinctive line of hills that sweeps east above Longnor, the eastern end being completed by Hitter Hill, Aldery Cliff and High Wheeldon.

Cross a lovely little stone footbridge into Derbyshire and ascend the bank, turning left

Hollinsclough with Chrome Hill behind

Brand End

along the freshly risen Dove after a gate and climbing up away from it to meet an old track at the top. Turn left and follow it north-northwest up through the gorse, with the sound of water below, past Fough Farm and on up to Booth Farm (2). Walk over the grid and take the stile in the fence on the left, walking behind the buildings northwest over stiles, through marsh grass, past a pond and down the valley at Brand End.

Cross a footbridge and keep straight on at the divergence of paths. Go through a gate and along a track, the brook below, still climbing. Reach a farm, Thirkelow Rocks above to the right, and then a lane at about 1,370ft (418m).

Turn left, then left again, west, down the track to Fairthorn Farm (3). Cross the stile just before the first building. Follow the building round, cross the stile into the garden and cross the stream by the footbridge. Climb south to the barn ahead and on to Birds Farm. Take the track up through the conifers and turn half-left after them, south-southeast. It is necessary to drop downhill to the left of the next house, skirt the garden and climb back to the stile.

Now continue south-southeast along the hillside to the next farm just over the brow. Turn right at the buildings, keeping them to the left, then fork left to the south-southwest. Walk down the right-hand of two gullies leading down to the valley bottom to find a footbridge across the Dove, most beautiful of all Peak District rivers, which rises just a short way above. You are now back in Staffordshire. Turn right and climb very steeply to Nether Colshaw Farm (4), keeping the buildings to the right and ascending the farm track ahead leading south.

Reach a lane and turn right and left, along a path leading south-southeast to the left-hand of two farms, passing to its right and continuing down to the whitewashed farm below. Pass to the left of that and continue southeast to the right of a half-ruined barn and east along a track to a stream, descending to cross it and rising to meet a lane.

Cross and continue south down a muddy farm track past Moseley Farm (5). At a fork turn left and walk northeast round Willshaw Hill. Descend to Willshaw Farm and then follow the sign towards Hilltop, climbing southeast and then south up the rim of the hill. Pass to the left of sadly abandoned Hill Top Farm, passing in front of the house and climbing the garden gate. Keep on south up to the gate on to the road.

Cross and take the track forking left (southeast), shortly turning right after a little quarried lay-by down a gorsey bank, over a stile and on south down a wall. Before a footbridge at the bottom (6) turn left over a stile and head east, climbing half-left to the left of a hawthorn thicket and continuing through gates towards a barn near some beech trees below a brackeny hillside ahead. Pass the barn and take the track east-southeast along the wall down to Ball Bank House Farm. Go through two gates and keep to the left of the farm buildings, forking left (east) steeply through

the bracken at the end of a long low barn.

Pass through a gateway and continue up the wall, over a stile and on to a lane. Turn left and cross the road to a stile. Chrome Hill is now in sight again ahead. Walk north across the fields to a lane and descend its dark, stony then grassy way back to the start.

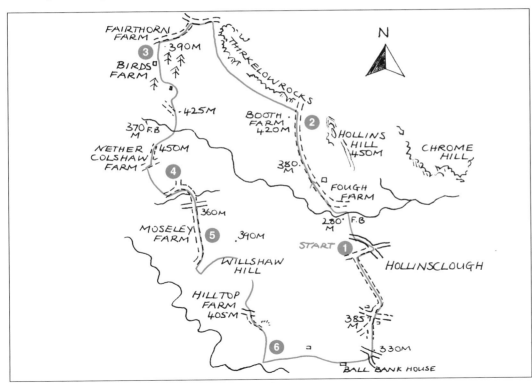

FACT FILE

Map OS Outdoor Leisure 24: The White Peak
Start/Finish SK 065665: Hollinsclough, which can be reached by bus
Length 7½ miles (12km)
Walking time 4 hours
Difficulty A couple of climbs, one very steep

The Route in Brief

1 SK 065665. Up through village, past farm, R down bridleway, across footbridge, L along river, and L up track to Booth Farm.

2 L after grid and NW down to footbridge. Straight on as path splits and up track to lane. L and L down track to Fairthorn Farm.

3 L over stiles down to footbridge and up to Birds Farm. Skirt next house and on SSE to farm over brow. R and down R of two gullies to footbridge. R and climb steeply up to farm.

4 Up farm track to lane. R and L down path SSE to L of 2 farms, past another farm, then barn, then E along track to cross stream. Cross lane and down track to farm.

5 L at fork to walk round hill to farm. Follow sign to Hilltop. L of farm and S up to road. Cross to track. R past little quarry down bank almost to footbridge.

6 L and E to barn, then ESE down track to farm. L at end of barn and E up hillside to lane. L and across road to path over fields and along lane down to start.

FLASH

The moorlands in Staffordshire's far northern tip provide wonderful walking, as this route demonstrates. It takes in woodland, rock formations, heather, a river, a mill, and farmland and pasture, and will satisfy all but the most demanding soul.

Lying at well over 1,500ft (460m), Flash claims to be the highest village in England, and it is certainly a bleak and exposed settlement in winter. Legend has it that counterfeit money used to be made here and that is was distributed by way of Three Shires Head, a beautiful spot a little to the northwest where Cheshire, Derbyshire and Staffordshire meet, the forgers therefore being able literally to step out of the jurisdiction of one county and into another if the law was about to catch up with them. The village thus gave its name to the adjective flash, as in 'flash Harry'. There is a shop and pub.

From the main road turn left in the village **(1)** and walk down the road for about three-quarters of a mile (1km). Just after a house on the left turn over a stile and descend some steps. Head down the wall and take the stile on the right in the opposite wall, crossing to another. Walk left down the track past Flash Brook Farm, hop over the brook by the footpath post and follow another brook and then a wall up south-southeast over a stile, through some heather and gently downhill, rocks to the right.

Reach Adder's Green Farm (2) and pass to the right of the buildings, Bald Stone Rocks visible ahead. Walk southwest along a path across pasture to a conifer plantation and go straight over the lane and along another. Gib Tor Farm is on the left, and just past its entrance turn right by the yellow arrow through the fir trees and along the inside of the wall on the edge of the wood. Gib Tor Rocks are to the northwest. Enter a nature reserve and follow the path as it curves round a set of rocks. Head south along the edge with Ramshaw Rocks and the Roaches in view ahead. Climb a stile out of the reserve and reach another formation of rocks (3).

Turn right down the road at Corner House past Newstone Farm and take a stile on the left to a path leading west. At a gap in the wall by a post fork right over the stile and follow the fence down northwest, Black Brook to the left, past Blackbank. At a footbridge fork right up a track and then left at a footpath sign to pass Goldsitch House. The way now becomes increasingly wild and lovely. Cross a track and head down to cross a brook and a stile. Descend into the valley along Black Brook, crossing it by a footbridge at the bottom (4).

Enter the National Park's Roaches Estate. The path climbs high up above and then away from the brook until it reaches and passes a farmhouse. A little further on there is a stile in the wall on the right. Cross this and descend north through the wood where wild bilberries grow.

You will come across a sign to Lud's Church and have the option to make a detour off the route to this deep, dank and gloomy cleft in the gritstone where the sun never shines. About 60ft (20m) high but very narrow, it may take its name from Walter de Ludank, a Lollard who met with others of his faith to worship here in the fourteenth century but was eventually arrested. There is a sense of secrecy and peace here, almost of magic, and it comes as no surprise to learn that it may have provided the setting for the Green Chapel which Sir Gawain sought in the medieval poem 'Sir Gawayne and the Grene Knight'. After inspecting Lud's Church continue in the same direction, turning right to descend through the woods to a footbridge and so to Gradbach Mill.

If you have not made the detour, carry on towards Gradbach, descending, steeply at times, through the beautiful woods. Pass a ford over Black Brook signed 'Gradbach' and

Opposite: Roach End with Shutlingsloe on the horizon
Right: The River Dane at Gradbach

89

Map OS Outdoor Leisure 24: The White Peak
Start/Finish SK 025672: Flash, which can be reached by bus
Length 8½ miles (13.5km), longer if you make the detour to Lud's Church
Walking time 4½ hours, longer if you make the detour to Lud's Church
Difficulty A couple of stiff pulls

The Route in Brief

1 SK 025672. From main road, L in village for ¾ mile (1km). L at path after house, down wall, and R over stile in opposite wall to another. L at track past farm, over brook and up another brook and wall SSE to Adder's Green Farm.
2 Pass to R of buildings and take path to conifers. Over lane and along another. R just past farm entrance through wood, into nature reserve, and along edge past rocks to stile at reserve boundary.
3 R at road, L at stile, R at post by gap in wall, down brook past Goldsitch House and down valley to cross brook at footbridge.
4 Climb above and away from brook to stile on R past farmhouse. Descend

wood (diverting to Lud's Church if wished), towards Gradbach, crossing brook by footbridge and reaching YH at mill.
5 E down road, L over footbridge, up river, R up lane, L at path, R over stile and NE up pasture. R down track before ladder stile, L up stream, L up wall, to R of farm, cross stream, and steeply up towards Flash, turning R up track, L over stile and L at lane.

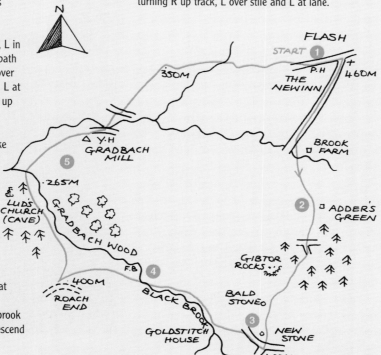

shortly cross a footbridge where the brook flows into the Dane river, which forms the border with Cheshire. Go left over a stile and follow the river up past Gradbach Mill, built in 1785 as a flax mill and now a Youth Hostel **(5)**.

Continue east along the road at the top of the drive down past the car park. Go left at the footpath sign over the footbridge, up the river, right up a lane and shortly left at another footpath sign. Fork right over a stile and walk up the field past an abandoned miniature house and on northeast up the wall of the pasture, picking up a track which runs out after a while, and on further. When the wall ends, continue northeast across the field to the next stile.

Just before the ladder stile in the next field turn right down a track, through gorse, to a stream. Turn left up it and shortly fork left up a wall away from it. The path now leads over a brick tip and passes to the right of a farm. Stay on the path as it descends to a footbridge over the stream and ascends steeply towards Flash. There are tremendous views behind to the west over the Dane valley. Turn right up a track, shortly left over a stile and left up the lane to Flash.

AROUND THE ROACHES

The distinctive shape of the line of gritstone rocks known as the Roaches is a familiar landmark to walkers of the southwest Peak, as well as being much favoured by rock climbers. This route in the far northern tip of Staffordshire circumnavigates it, from south to north in an anti-clockwise direction, enjoying the best of some high, windswept terrain and the lusher and more sheltered pasture of the valley to its west.

From the car park on the northeast shore of Tittesworth Reservoir **(1)**, from where a minibus service operates to the Roaches on summer weekends, take the track north back to the road and turn right. At Middle Hulme Farm, after the big bend to the right, take the track leading east. At a sharp bend continue straight over a stile and a path, cross a brook and follow along it to a stile. The Ordnance Survey map is misleading here. Turn left, signed 'Upper Hulme', then right, through a farm, turning right down the lane into the village.

As you face the little waterfall (a weir) in the middle of Upper Hulme **(2)**, there is a concrete path to your right leading north. Take this, passing through the gate at the end of the buildings, and follow the path past the ruin of Dains Mill and, very boggily, up the brook. The path leads left-handed round a rocky outcrop and over a stile. Take the track to the right leading off the white gravelled track. The heather begins here, and there are views of Ramshaw Rocks to the northeast and of Hen Cloud rising to 1,345ft (410m) behind the trees to the west. Ahead to the northwest is the southern tip of the Roaches, which rise to 1,657ft (505m) at their northern end.

Keep right when the track divides **(3)**, with well-named Ferny Knowl Farm to the east. Having climbed the stile at the start of the wall, ignore the track which leads through the gate in the fence ahead and instead head north towards the far end of the same fence and broken wall to a stile. Do not now climb half-left to the stile situated in the fenced wall but continue straight on to the stile under the sycamores **(4)**.

You are now on the Staffordshire Moorlands Walk. Cross the stream and continue up the other side of the brackeny valley. You will soon see a farm ahead and above, with another on your left. Cross the footbridge and shortly after take a less-distinct path to the left which soon peters out. Head across the patch of rough ground to find a stile by the telegraph pole below the farm ahead.

Go through the gate by the farmhouse. The path runs between the fence and the hedge and through the gate ahead. Respect the owners' privacy. Follow the track until it shortly bends to the right. Fork left up the wall, past a gate and stile and along the fence, following the waymarkers. There are marvellous views to the north ahead, often accompanied by the 'go-back, go-back' of the red grouse.

Skirt Shawtop Farm **(5)** and leave on the farm track, turning left on to the road above Shaw Farm. Cross the cattle grid into the Roaches Estate and head north, passing Shawside Farm and looking ahead towards the distant hills. The road rises to over 1,400ft (425m) before beginning to fall.

We now leave the Staffordshire Moorlands Walk. At the sharp left-hand bend, where a track leads down to Lower Roach End Farm, go straight ahead along a path **(6)**, heading northwest. Tittesworth Reservoir reveals itself to the south, while to the west there are quite sensational views across Cheshire to the hills of north Wales. The path descends, then climbs. Fork left, signed 'Danebridge', then

left again, signed 'Clough Head', heading south with the reservoir in the distance. Walk along the farm track until forking half-right at the cattle grid, across the field to the lane. Turn right past the farm and down to the next **(7)**. There is a stile in the wall (overgrown on my last visit) just after the gate into the farm and another stile opposite leading across the pasture to a farm track heading south-southwest. Follow it down to a gate, the Roaches and Hen Cloud now in view to the southeast. A path leads along the fence through some trees and over a stile by a gate. Go left at the sign and over a series of fields and stiles leading south towards Meadows Farm **(8)**.

Now continue south along the track, keeping on where another comes in from the right. After the next cattle grid, by a brook, cut across the pasture half-right to a stile in the corner and on up the hedge. Cross a track to a footbridge and a gate leading through two farms. Follow the hedge and wall south, through the

Left: Towards the Roaches
Right: Hen Cloud

next gate, straight on over the farm lane and up the track ahead. Where a sign points straight on to Meerbrook fork left down a track. At a telegraph pole fork right to a stile in the hedge. Glimpse the church at Meerbrook. It was built in Victorian times to Norman Shaw's design and is an excellent example of his work. The reservoir claimed half the village, but a pub and a youth hostel remain.

Slant left across the field to the lane. Turn left then immediately right down the track towards Frith Bottom Farm. This is the Staffordshire Moorlands Walk again. Just before the farm **(9)** turn right over stiles and across pasture to a stile in the far fenced hedge where it bends. Meerbrook church is again visible to the right. Follow signs and markers across the fields towards Hen Cloud, turning half-right at a stone barn to a stile in the field corner.

Fork right at the brook, leaving Benthead Farm to the left. Now cross a series of stiles south over fields to the gate at Middle Hulme Farm. Turn right at the lane and retrace your steps back to the car park.

Map OS Outdoor Leisure 24: The White Peak
Start/Finish SK 994603: car park on NE shore of Tittesworth Reservoir. There are buses to nearby Meerbrook
Length 9 miles (14.5km)
Walking time 5 hours
Difficulty Easy enough on the whole. A compass would be useful

The Route in Brief

1 SK 994603. Take track to road, R to farm, E along track, continuing straight on at bend to Upper Hulme.

2 Take concrete path (on R as you face waterfall) N, giving on to path leading past Dains Mill. Track to R off gravelled track.

3 R when track divides, over stile, N to far end of fence and broken wall to stile and straight on to stile under sycamores.

4 Cross brook and N to footbridge. Across rough ground to stile by telegraph pole below farm. Past farm, up track, L up wall, past gate and stile and along fence to Shawtop Farm.

5 Up farm track and L at road. Straight ahead along path at sharp L bend.

6 L towards Danebridge, L towards Clough Head. Along track, ½R at grid across field, R down lane to 2nd farm.

7 Stile in wall to another, then farm track to gate. Path along fence through trees then over fields and stiles S to Meadows Farm.

8 S along tracks and paths till L where sign says straight on to Meerbrook. R over hedge stile and L across field to lane. L then R down track towards Frith Bottom Farm.

9 Follow SMW signs: R before farm, over stiles, towards Hen Cloud, ½R at stone barn to stile in field corner. R at brook, S over fields to road and back to start.

94

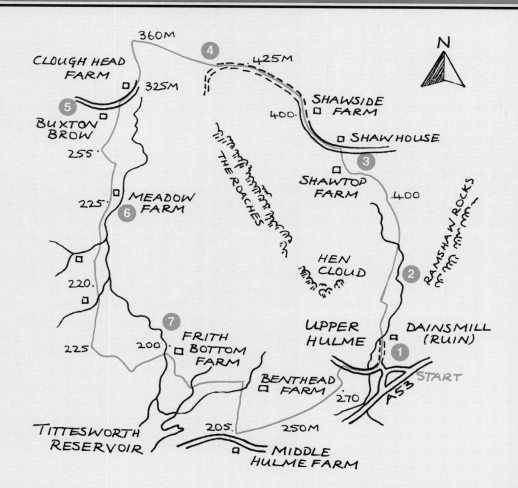

THE MERMAID

This true moorland route requires a compass. The walker will cross some tough heathery terrain with no path to follow but will be rewarded with a richly satisfying day and some lovely views in this lonely and bleak corner of Staffordshire. Do not attempt the walk if the army ranges are in very occasional use. (Red warning flags will fly. Ring the army in Leek to check, tel: 01538-300457.) In any event, do not stray into the military area.

The isolated old drovers' inn, the Mermaid, is so called after Blake Mere, sometimes known as the Mermaid's Pool, to the north. The lady concerned is said to appear at midnight and drown in the bottomless waters anyone so unwise as to be lurking in such a desolate spot at such an hour.

Take the path to the left of the car park **(1)**, with excellent views of Hen Cloud, the Roaches and Ramshaw Rocks to the northwest, and follow the fence down to the gates. The path follows the brook down north-northwest. Ford the brooks where they meet. Go through a gate and climb the pasture, taking a stile to the right of a barn and heading to the right-hand of two gates in the next field. Cut off the corner of the next to a gate before a black corrugated iron barn at Little Swainsmoor Farm. Pass through the yard and head along the track leading northwest to Swainsmoor Farm **(2)**.

Walk through the yard and, as tracks fork left and right, continue straight ahead, northerly, across the pasture to a Ministry of Defence notice and on to a bend in the stream. Cross a stile, ford the stream, a tributary of the young River Churnet, and turn right up it, soon crossing a brook by a stone footbridge. Turn left and head east-northeast up between the wooded brook and the fenced wall on the right to a stile in a fence. Cross this and continue straight ahead to some marshy ground and walk northeast with a broken wall on the left. Spare a moment to look back southwest over Leek to the distant hills.

Walk up to a group of stunted sycamores and follow the stream up to the fence, keeping on the right side of the little clough. Cross the stream **(3)** and then the fence, and continue

Boarsgrove Farm

95

FACT FILE

Map OS Outdoor Leisure 24: The White Peak
Start/Finish SK 037604: the Mermaid Inn, which
can be reached by bus
Length 6 miles (9.5km)
Walking time 3½ hours or more
Difficulty A compass is vital for navigation across the
moors. Do not attempt the walk when visibility is bad.
Several streams must be forded, so waterproof boots
should be worn

The Route in Brief

1 SK 037604. Take path to L
of car park down fence, then
signed path NNW. Ford
where brooks meet and
climb to stile to R of barn
and so to Little
Swainsmoor Farm.
2 Through yard and
straight ahead past MoD
notice to bend in
stream. Ford and turn
R, crossing brook. L
up between brook and
wall to stile. Over
marshy ground NE to
sycamores. Up R side of
clough to fence and
across stream.

3 Cross fence. NE up fence, following round N and
taking track ENE at its end, keeping R at fork.
4 Cross road and E across moor to Boarsgrove Farm.
Out on track L on to road. R on to moor by stake and
S to stile halfway up wall. Cross corner of field to stile
and on to farm.
5 R at road, L down track, R up track before farm and
down to brook. SW over stiles up to road. L and fork R
back to pub.

northeast between the stream on the right and
the army-range fence with red DANGER notices
on it. Walk through the heather, crossing the
stream again.

Follow the fence when it turns 90° to the left
and walk northerly, once again crossing the
stream. At the end of it, near Dry Stones,
swing right with the track and head east-
northeast, keeping right at the fork. Cross the
road (4). You should be able to see a barn, part
of Boarsgrove Farm, on the distant hillside.
Head due east across the heather, crossing a
stream, to this farm. Eventually, just under it,
gain a track leading past a small waterfall and
up through the farm, leaving on the track to
the road.

Turn left and step right on to the moor
where you shortly see a wooden stake. Head
south, coming off the heather over a stile into
a field halfway up a fenced wall, crossing the
corner of the field to the next stile and
continuing to Round Knowl Farm.

Turn right at the road and left down the
track towards Noon Sun Farm (5), going right
up the track just before it. Follow it west down
to a brook, then cross the stile ahead and
continue southwest over more stiles. Cross the
fence by the remains of a barn and head up the
rough pasture to the road. From here there are
stunning views southeast back to the Manifold
Valley with Hazelton Clump standing sentinel
beyond. Turn left at the road, the Mermaid's
Pool on the right, and fork right back to the
Mermaid Inn.

LATHKILL AND BRADFORD DALES

This is a relatively straightforward, easy walk, descending from the tops to Lathkill Dale, one of the most famous dales in Derbyshire, skirting the attractive town of Youlgreave, and returning by Bradford Dale, surely one of the most underrated in the Peak.

From the Moor Lane picnic area **(1)**, turn left up the road and take the footpath straight ahead at the junction. This is the Limestone Way, and it leads west-southwest. Pass Calling Low Farm, and note the fine buildings of One Ash Grange Farm standing out across the valley. Both establishments were owned by monasteries in the Middle Ages and used for wool production. Monks who had erred at Roche Abbey in Yorkshire are said to have been confined in the latter.

Descend steeply **(2)** into Cales Dale and turn right at the bottom. Cross the footbridge and turn right along Lathkill Dale, walking east along it. The Lathkill River is possibly the purest river in England. In winter it emerges from a cave in the hillside a few hundred yards/metres northwest up the valley, but in dry weather it flows underground for the first two miles (3km) or more. Charles Cotton wrote that it is 'by many degrees, the purest and most transparent stream that I ever saw, either at home or abroad, and breeds, it is said, the reddest and the best Trouts in England'.

The dale was for many centuries the site of extensive lead mining, despite problems of flooding, and this is the probable reason for the river's disappearing act. It is now a National Nature Reserve.

Lathkill Lodge is the point where in dry weather the river suddenly appears in all its considerable beauty, soon gathering strength. The water is sparklingly clear and teeming with fish. Turn right at the road over Conksbury Bridge **(3)**. This was once the high road from Bakewell across to the Newhaven Inn and Ashbourne, and this old bridge must have witnessed some important comings and goings in time gone by. Turn left at the footpath leading past charming Raper Lodge. (Those that are in need of sustenance should continue a little way up the road to Conksbury Farm where, in season, they will find the best home-made tea in Derbyshire.)

Lathkill Dale

Alport
An ancient bridge over the Bradford

The path leads southeast to Alport, an attractive old lead-mining village, where the Lathkill joins the Bradford, and the two flow on together to meet the Wye below Haddon Hall. The Portway passes over the packhorse bridge on its ancient route from Nottingham to Castleton. Cross the road and river and walk southwest down Bradford Dale.

The Bradford, like the Lathkill, rises on limestone and is spectacularly pure and clear. It surprised everyone in early 1881 by suddenly disappearing after heavy floods caused some disused lead mines to collapse, flowing underground on an altered course to Darley Dale. Happily it later reverted to its old bed where it remains. Cross the road on the outskirts of Youlgreave village, and then the river at Bradford Dams near Meadow Cottage café (4).

Youlgreave is well worth exploring. It is a large and lively village with some fine buildings, including the handsome church, and some pubs and shops. The parish register tells of 'the greatest snow which ever fell upon the Earth within man's memorye'. On 16 January 1614 it began, covering the ground to a depth of some 45in (110cm): 'And for heapes, or drifts of snow, they were very deap so that passengers, both horse and foot, passed over gates, hedges and walles.' It lasted until the end of May, to be followed the next year by a great drought, only three showers falling between 25 March and 4 August.

The next stretch of the river is almost incomparably pretty and peaceful. Trout are easy to spy in the clear pools, and there are grebes, dippers and wagtails, not to mention mallards, coots, water voles and moorhens.

Keep on, following the river as it bends south, eventually passing through a gate and soon crossing over an old stone bridge at a footpath sign, less than a mile (1.5km) from Bradford Dams. Climb steeply up away from the river and turn right at the road.

Pass nineteenth-century Lomberdale Hall, where the famous Derbyshire archaeologist Thomas Bateman lived. His tomb is in a field a little to the south. As the road bends turn left through a stile by a gate and climb up to another road. Turn left after the bend and right up a footpath, crossing a series of stiles leading west and north back to the start.

FACT FILE

Map OS Outdoor Leisure 24: The White Peak
Start/Finish SK 194644: picnic area at Moor Lane. There are buses from nearby Youlgreave
Length 8 miles (13km)
Walking time At least 4 hours, more if you visit Youlgreave
Difficulty A steep descent and a less steep ascent, otherwise easy

The Route in Brief

1 SK 194644. L at road to footpath ahead at junction and WSW to Cales Dale.
2 R at bottom, over bridge and R (E) down Lathkill Dale.
3 R at road over Conksbury

Bridge and L at path to Alport. SW along River Bradford, crossing road outside Youlgreave and river at Bradford Dams.
4 W then S along Bradford Dale to stone bridge. Cross and climb to road. R then L up path to next road. L after bend then R up path back to start.

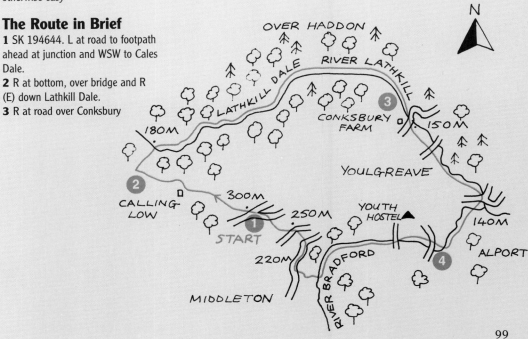

99

LONGNOR AND THE MANIFOLD

This walk of considerable contrasts begins at the remote uplands Staffordshire village of Longnor, then heads south along the valley of the Manifold River before climbing up on to moorland and turning back northwest across lovely farm and pasture land to the start.

Standing on a ridge between the Dove and Manifold Rivers, and at a turnpike crossing, Longnor, though only the size of a village, has the satisfying air of a town. Indeed, until fairly recent times it was a bustling and important centre with regular markets and fairs. It still comes as a charming surprise in the midst of some of the loveliest and loneliest hill country in England. The churchyard contains the grave of William Billinge who died at the age of 112 in 1791. Though he led an exciting life, and was wounded at the Battle of Ramilles in 1706 under the Duke of Marlborough, he died, his gravestone tells us 'within a space of 150 yards from where he

Longnor village

was born'. It is remarkable to think that as a child he could have met someone born in Queen Elizabeth I's reign, and as an old man would have known a generation who would live well into the age of the railways, telescoping time. There are shops, inns, and accommodation in Longnor.

Leave the centre of the village **(1)** on the Sheen road. Do not take the footpath opposite the Cheshire Cheese pub but the one to the right some yards after. Head through Folds End farmyard and turn south towards the river. The Manifold is still a young river here, having risen west-northwest of Longnor on the moors just south of Axe Edge. It is lined by alders and beech trees and the path runs alongside, the ground rising to the southeast. Before Lower Boothlow Farm turn round and admire the view back up the valley to Longnor with the hills in the distance.

Cross a brook and keep just to the left of the barn between Lower Boothlow and Frog Hole farms, just two of a lovely sequence of valley farmsteads. Sheen Hill (1,247ft/380m) comes into view to the east before Ridge End Farm, shortly after which turn right **(2)** and head west down a green lane where foxgloves and scabious grow, to a footbridge over the Manifold. Turn left here and head southwest

across stiles to the minor road. Turn left again and continue southwest over the brook to the junction.

Turn right for a short distance and then left at the footpath, heading southwest up to and across the B5053. Suddenly the terrain becomes rougher, moorlike, with heather and gorse springing up around you. Look back as you climb towards the summit (over 1,000ft/305m). The views north, east and south sweep through 180° across the Manifold valley and its surrounding hills, from Longnor in the north towards Alstonefield in the southeast.

Turn left over the stile towards Knowle Farm for a few steps, then slant right, walking southwest past a tiny abandoned house, climbing gently past a small farm, then dropping equally gently straight on to the road **(3)**. Now a new vista to the west opens up. The Butcher's Arms, a lonely but convivial free house, is a few hundred yards north along the road.

Go straight over the road, taking the path which leads northwest downhill past a small barn, and on down parallel with a track but on the other side of the fence to cross Blake Brook at a footbridge. Continue northwest over a stile across another brook. Now, with the farm

at Smedley Sytch to your left and west, and a small barn to your right and east, walk northwest up the hedge and, when it ends, head for the far northwest corner of the field to find a stile by a brook. Now head due north uphill to Boosley Grange **(4)**.

Skirt to the right of the buildings, then fork left (northwest), keeping in the same direction at a junction of paths and descending through marshy ground to a brook. Now climb to handsome Newtown House (1620), which may contain the core of an earlier house associated with the Beresford family, and turn right (north) up the track to the road. Turn left for a few paces, then right up the drive of Holly Grove Farm, passing through the coalyard to a stile.

Descend the pasture and cross the stile at a patch of boggy ground. Find a stile in the wall on the left by the second gate and head north-northeast towards the stile on to the lane. Turn left up the lane over Oakenclough Brook at Shining Ford **(5)** (do not cross the footbridge). Round the bend and take the stile by the footpath sign on the right. Now head northeast, hugging the wall, crossing the field to the wall ahead and then hugging that, the brook running roughly parallel to the east. High Wheeldon (1,383ft/422m) looms ahead to the northeast.

Follow the path, then a track, with conifers

The Manifold valley below Longnor

on the hills to the east, through the farm. Turn right on to the road and walk east. After some 600 yards/metres go through a gate on the left, just before a stand of sycamores on the right. Head northeast down the pasture towards a line of trees at the bottom of the valley. Cross the footbridge over Oakenclough Brook and keep northeast along the path towards Fawside Farm in the distance, a pleasing mixed wood on the right.

Walk through the farmyard (6) and along the track beyond, shortly forking right along the footpath leading east to Longnor. Admire the skyline range of hills to the east of the village on both sides of the Dove valley leading down to Pilsbury. Flat-topped Sheen Hill is to the southeast and High Wheeldon to the northeast. Cross the little brook and gain the lane by Gauledge Farm leading into Longnor. A superb vista of the hills to the south opens up, including distinctive Wetton Hill, guarding the entrance to the lower Manifold valley.

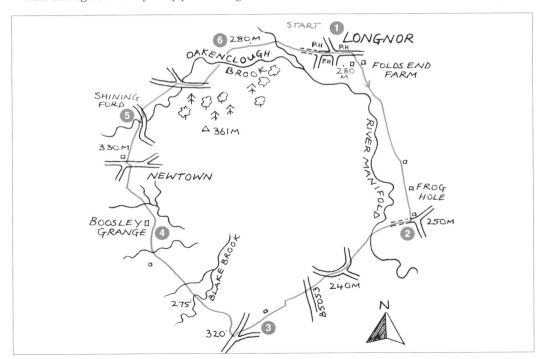

FACT FILE

Map OS Outdoor Leisure 24: The White Peak
Start/Finish SK 088648: Longnor, which can be reached by bus
Length 7³/₄ miles (12.5km)
Walking time 4¹/₂ hours
Difficulty A compass would be useful

The Route in Brief

1 SK 088648. Sheen road out of village. Take 2nd path on R after Cheshire Cheese through Folds End Farm and S down Manifold valley.
2 R after Ridge End Farm to footbridge. L over stiles to road and L to junction. R, then L at path, across B5053, up across moor, L then immediately R and SW to road.
3 Straight over and NW down across brook, across another and on to stile by a 3rd. N up to Boosley Grange.
4 NW down across brook then up to Newtown House and N up track to Holly Grove Farm. Down across pastures NNE to Shining Ford.
5 L up lane over brook, round bend, and take path on R. NE to farm by road. R, then L down path NE to Fawside Farm.
6 E along path then lane to Longnor.

HARTINGTON AND PILSBURY CASTLE

The River Dove here neatly divides the limestone of the White Peak and the gritstone of the Dark. This walk, with many fine viewpoints, takes advantage of both terrains, ascending north through open, airy pasture along the gritstone edge north of Hartington village, then descending back to the river and the ancient fort at Pilsbury, finally returning along a farm track and up the limestone slopes below Carder Low.

Hartington stands at over 700ft (213m), is surrounded by lovely country and boasts a wealth of fine limestone cottages and houses. It was an important market centre throughout the Middle Ages and still attracts plenty of custom from those living in the locality. Tourists flock to it during the summer and it sometimes seems in danger of losing its identity; but in the close season it reverts to its traditional and quieter ways. There are facilities of all sorts, and the most

impressive Youth Hostel you are likely to encounter at Hartington Hall, a classic Jacobean manor house, for many centuries the home of the Bateman family.

From the centre of the village **(1)** follow the signpost to Pilsbury and turn left up the lane marked 'No Through Road'. The Stilton cheese factory lies ahead. Stilton may only be made in Leicestershire, Nottinghamshire and Derbyshire, and it has been made in Hartington for some 120 years. Turn right along the footpath in front of the factory and follow it northwest over stiles and meadows – spangled with buttercups and clover in the spring and summer – gently downhill to the River Dove. This is the county border. Cross the river into Staffordshire and head up the field towards the gateway ahead. The contrast between the limestone and gritstone country can be seen in the colour of the walls.

Turn right along the track **(2)** and, after 100 yards/metres, left up a steep bank through thorn and gorse bushes and then through the top edge of a wood of Scots pine and larch. Sheen village is visible to the left. Continue along the top of the field, with fine views of the valley, farmsteads and Hartington behind, and, as likely as not, the sound of curlews crying on the wind. Cross the stile at the

Left: Pilsbury Castle with Chrome and Parkhouse hills in the distance. Far right: Hartington

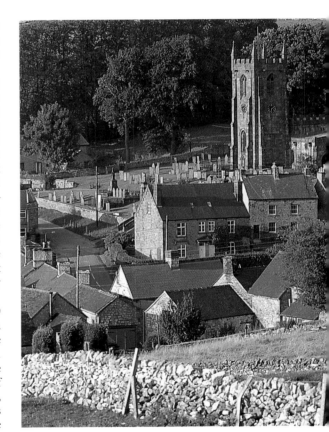

The way back from Pilsbury Castle

junction of three walls and continue, now at just under 1,000ft (305m), with more superb views, northwest over fields and stiles, to Harris Close Farm.

Turn right on to the road **(3)** and right again at the fingerpost after 300 yards/metres. Above, Sheen Hill rises to 1,247ft (380m).

Pass the farm and descend diagonally across the fields and stiles in a northerly direction. Broadmeadow Hall, dark and brooding, on the Staffordshire side of the river, contrasts starkly with the lighter stone of the farm buildings at the hamlet of Pilsbury ahead in Derbyshire. At the bottom of the valley meet a track leading down to the river. This is the old Brund to Pilsbury road, formerly known as the Salt Way, and it is easy to imagine the

packhorses and carts lumbering down to the shallow ford in days gone by.

Cross the river by the footbridge **(4)**, walk up towards the farm, turn left at the road and carry straight on northerly along the track where the road turns right. This leads to Pilsbury Castle, last used by the Normans as one of their bases, possibly for the 'Wasting of the North' in the late 1060s, and now just a series of grassed-over motte-and-bailey earthworks. The site was almost certainly in use as a stronghold long before Norman times, and there is a very ancient feeling about it. A pinnacle of limestone stands guard over the whole, its shape a miniature version of the peaks of Chrome and Parkhouse hills rising above Longnor in the distance to the northwest.

Return along the track (5) to the farm buildings at Pilsbury and walk south along the gated farm lane ahead, through a cool grove of sycamores and horse chestnuts and over a gushing spring towards mysterious Ludwell Mill, where once bones were crushed for meal. Turn left up the track before the mill (6). Swing left towards the small barn, then right through the gateway, and left and right past the hummocks (the remains of an old lead mine) to the stile in the wall on the right. (Do not take the stile in the wall above the hummocks.) The view behind, northwest, beyond Pilsbury Castle to Hitter, Chrome and Parkhouse hills, is one of the most entrancing in the White Peak.

Continue south across the stony fields, following yellow markers, to a gateway in the far wall. The path leads from the right of the gateway along a grassy natural terrace above Bank Top Farm. Turn left up the farm track, then cross fields and stiles to the road (7). Turn right here (south), then right just before the white cottage, southwest down a green lane, and left at the bottom and back into Hartington village.

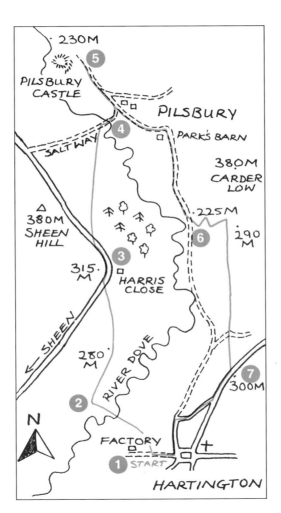

FACT FILE

Map OS Outdoor Leisure 24: The White Peak
Start/Finish SK 128604: Hartington, which can be reached by bus
Length 5½ miles (9km)
Walking time 4 hours, depending on time spent at Pilsbury Castle
Difficulty Easy grassy hills, tracks and lanes. Two short, stiff ascents

The Route in Brief

1 SK 128604. Follow 'Pilsbury' sign, then L up 'No Through Road' to factory. R in front of factory. Descend NW to, and cross, river.

2 R at track, then L up bank, N along top of wood and NW up through fields.

3 R on to road, then walk NW, turning R again after 300 yards/metres at fingerpost. Diagonally N down fields to track to river.

4 Cross river and turn L on to road. Straight on N along track to Pilsbury Castle.

5 Retrace tracks to farm buildings at Pilsbury. Follow lane S.

6 Take track L up bank after spring and before farm. Follow around the mine hummocks and take stile to R of (not above) them. Follow yellow markers S across fields, turn L at track and cross fields S to road.

7 R (S) at road, then R (SW) down green lane opposite white cottage and back into village.

WOLFSCOTE AND BERESFORD DALES

These two dales of the River Dove are justifiably among the most celebrated in the Peak but, despite their popularity, have not yet suffered the overcrowded fate of Dovedale. The route also visits the villages of Alstonefield and Hartington and returns to the former 'over the tops'.

From the car park (1) in Alstonefield turn right through a stile, cross the field, turn right into a lane and walk straight on, northeast over the meadows. Cross a track, head up another, pass a barn and descend Gipsy Bank, which is very steep and sometimes slippery. At the River Dove cross the stepping stones into Derbyshire. These may be treacherous or indeed under water when the river is high. If that is the case, turn right down the bank to Coldeaton Bridge, cross there and return up the other side of the river. Otherwise cross by the stones, turn left

Wolfscote Dale and the River Dove

and walk north-northwest up the river through Wolfscote Dale.

Wolfscote is said to mean 'Wulfstan's cottage'. I prefer to think of it as referring to the wolves who once scraped a living here before being hunted to extinction. Biggin Dale, a dry dale, shortly comes in from the right, while opposite are Peaseland Rocks and the pointed buttress of Drabber Tor. Eventually you will reach a footbridge. Do not cross this but keep on over the meadow ahead and cross the next footbridge (2) back into Staffordshire.

This is Beresford Dale, tiny and exquisite, and not taking its name, I am sure, from 'Bear's Ford' as I always believed, referring to the last bear to be slain in England. Shortly cross another footbridge back to the east bank. This famous stretch of water is known as the Pike Pool and is guarded by a tall, thin spire, or pike, of rock. It still looks today as inviting as it did to Charles Cotton, the writer and translator of Montaigne, who introduced his friend Izaak Walton to the delights of the Pool and the Dove in general. He also contributed a treatise on fly-fishing to the fifth edition of *The Compleat Angler* (1676). He

was a hard-living and extravagant gentleman, and was eventually forced to sell his ancestral home of Beresford Hall which then stood just across the river on the Staffordshire bank. He built the very charming Fishing House (no access) which can be glimpsed in the trees to the left as the river swings away from the path. Here he spent many happy hours smoking his pipe, regretting his excesses, and ruminating on the habits and foibles of the brown trout.

To Cotton this part of the world, and the Dove in particular, was a calming antidote to his reckless London life:

Good God! how sweet are all things here!
How beautiful the fields appear!
    How cleanly do we feed and lie!
Lord! What good hours do we keep!
How quietly we sleep!
    What peace, what unanimity!
How innocent from the lewd fashion
Is all our business, all our recreation!

Walkers and fishermen alike, to whom the 'princess of rivers' is still sacred, find a special enchantment in Beresford Dale.

Continue north as the pasture rises gently

past steep little Pennilow Hill and across a track to reach a road **(3)** on the outskirts of Hartington (see Walk 30), where there are pubs, tea-rooms and shops, first glimpsing the green glint of Sheen church on the northwest horizon. Cross to the stile opposite and walk through the farm, the Stilton cheese factory to the right. Head southwest across stiles and fields to where the river flows under the road at the mill at Hartington Bridge, still forming the county boundary.

Cross the bridge and turn right at the footpath. Climb steeply past Banktop, looking back to admire the view to Hartington across the river and weir. Pass a house and descend the drive of a farm to a lane, the trig point to the right standing at 873ft (266m). Turn left, then left at the path on the bend with a fine view of the glorious line of hills ranging east from Wetton Hill and jostling for supremacy. (This section of the route can be by-passed by turning right on to the road by the mill and walking along it to take the footpath on the left some way after the gates of old Beresford Hall.)

Descend to and cross the road and head south over the brook **(4)** and on to Lower Hurst Farm, keeping to the left of the buildings. It is here that some of the finest free-range beef in the district is reared. Skirt the left edge of the wood ahead and, crossing

Beresford Dale near Hartington

the brook, the right edge of the next wood. Turn right at the lane and shortly left down the path, then drive, to Field House Farm, passing to the right and continuing down the track. This stretch is often muddy. Follow stiles across the fields, past a barn, and down an exceptionally muddy track, over a brook, and up a track to the left of Narrowdale Farm. Turn left down the next track **(5)** and shortly after, where the tracks diverge, turn right through the gate up Narrowdale.

Soon fork right up an indistinct path which doubles back steeply up Narrowdale Hill and curls round southwest to a stile in a wall before continuing up the side of the hill. Keep on south across a track by Greenhills Farm and reach a lane. Double back along the wall in the same field and turn right over a wall-stile. Now follow stiles across the fields south-southeast back to Alstonefield (see Walk 33), where there is a fine pub, a shop and also a tea-room.

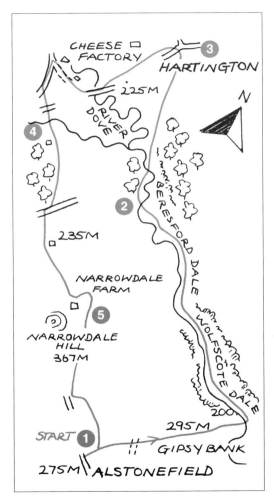

FACT FILE

Map OS Outdoor Leisure 24: The White Peak
Start/Finish SK 131556: car park at Alstonefield, which can be reached by bus
Length 8¼ miles (13km), longer if the Coldeaton Bridge crossing of the Dove is taken downstream from Gipsy Bank
Walking time 5 hours
Difficulty Waterproof boots should be worn to cross the stepping stones and to deal with some muddy stretches. There is a steep descent and a couple of steep climbs

The Route in Brief

1 SK 131556. R through stile opposite car park, across field, R into lane and straight on over fields, across track, up another and steeply down Gipsy Bank to river. Across stepping stones, or downstream to bridge, up other side of river, past footbridge, and over meadow to cross next bridge.
2 Up through Beresford Dale and N to road at Hartington.
3 Cross to stile opposite and SW to mill at road. Cross bridge and R up path past houses. Descend drive and L at lane. L at bend to road. Cross and head S to footbridge.
4 Past farm and skirt edges of 2 woods. R at lane and L down path, then drive, past farm, and SSE down track, across fields, down track, across brook, up track to L of farm and L down next track.
5 R up Narrowdale and shortly R up hill, eventually to stile in wall. S across track by farm to lane. Double back along wall to stile then SSE back to Alstonefield.

THE MANIFOLD VALLEY

This enchanting walk visits two particularly attractive Staffordshire villages and dips down into the Manifold valley at the very point where the river famously disappears underground. It climbs steeply through Ladyside Wood, as lovely a spot as anywhere in the White Peak, and returns to its beginning across rough pasture typical of this part of the Staffordshire Moorlands.

Butterton village is a gem, tumbling attractively downhill to a long ford at the bottom. Its stone has indeed a soft honey or butter colour to it which entirely suits its name and would not look out of place in the Cotswolds. A headless horseman is said to ride a white horse along the nearby Onecote–Warslow road and down the Manifold valley on moonlit nights.

Walk to the bottom of the village (1), where there is a pub and a shop; leaving it, turn left halfway along the ford, then right before a

Left: The ford at Butterton
Opposite: Thor's Cave

house and across a stream. This is the Hoo Brook, busy but secretive, on its way to meet the River Manifold. Follow the often muddy path southeast downstream. Soon cross a small tributary, then the brook itself, continuing along the northern bank through meadows which are spangled with wild flowers in spring and summer.

Where paths meet, near a footbridge, turn left along the brook and walk northeast and then east gently downhill through Waterslacks ('wet hollow') to meet the river at Wetton Mill. Here refreshments are available during the season. It has become a popular spot in recent years and you are unlikely to be alone. It fell into disuse as a mill in the mid nineteenth century. The cave in Nan Tor above was used by Mesolithic Man. The Manifold river goes underground below the Mill in dry weather to reappear above Ilam. Its near neighbour and partner the Hamps does a similar disappearing act.

Turn right along the lane **(2)** running parallel to the old railway line and river and turn right over the bridge where the roads meet. The Manifold Valley Light Railway once ran along this route between Waterhouses and Hulme End. It was never a success, partly because, as someone once pointed out, 'it starts nowhere and finishes up at same place'. Opened in 1904, it was closed some 30 years later. Now continue along the west bank of the river until, where a footbridge crosses it, you will see the mouth of Thor's Cave high in the

A tumulus on Grindon Moor

opposite hillside. If you wish to visit it cross the bridge and take the steep and often slippery path and then steps up 250ft (75m) above the valley.

Though the cave, named after the Norse god of thunder, has never been thoroughly excavated, it has yielded some interesting remains of early man, dating back to Neolithic and Mesolithic times. It was originally part of a subterranean river system of caverns and similar to what may now exist underneath the Hamps and Manifold rivers. It is best visited on a summer's evening when the light floods in from the west and the view from the mouth reveals the Manifold valley in all its considerable glory, every bit as inspiring as its more famous neighbour Dovedale.

Climb back down to and cross the bridge. Take the footpath ahead (or turn right if you have stayed in the valley), westerly up through Ladyside Wood. There are few more beautiful spots than this when the sun is slanting through the trees, and you are advised to linger. At a stile in a wall, emerge from the wood and take the footpath southwest along the right-hand side of the brook. The spire of Grindon church, which shows itself as a splendid landmark from all sorts of unexpected places throughout this area, hoves into view. Cross a stile after the footpath has

risen away from the brook, then cross the brook **(3)** and climb into Grindon.

Like its neighbour Butterton, Grindon is surprisingly little known, and all the better for that. It is as pretty as a picture. The church, built in 1848 by the Francis brothers on a much older site, is tasteful and subdued, and is sometimes known as the 'Cathedral of the Staffordshire Moorlands'. The Cavalier public house understands the needs of walkers.

Turn right in the village, walk round the church, keeping it to your right, and take the left of two stiles. For the next stretch of the walk head west then west-northwest. Cross a large field, aiming 100 yards/metres to the right of the far left corner, cross a stile, walk up the narrowing field to the stile in the top right corner and cross the next two fields, keeping just in from the road. This footpath is little used and may be overgrown. Cross the stile on to the road at the left-hand end of the second field. This is Grindonmoor Gate **(4)**.

Cross the road to the stile opposite, cross the small paddock and drive and continue west-northwest out into the fields. This is now classic Staffordshire Moorlands country, more open and less obviously pretty than Derbyshire's beauty-spots, but every bit as satisfying. Cross broken walls towards Sheldon Farm ahead, taking the stile in the remaining high wall. Just before the farm the footpath turns acutely right, though it may not be distinct, bending back on itself to cross the stile in the wall on to the road, which you cross.

The height here is above 1,200ft (365m) and there are fine views north towards Butterton, which lies below. Cross the tumuli (5) to the gate on to the track, then the stile at the footpath sign and head down the wall. Cross the stile ahead and aim for the left of the barns. Cross the yard and find the stile to the right of the fence directly ahead. Now head down the fields for a thoroughly enjoyable stroll back to Butterton.

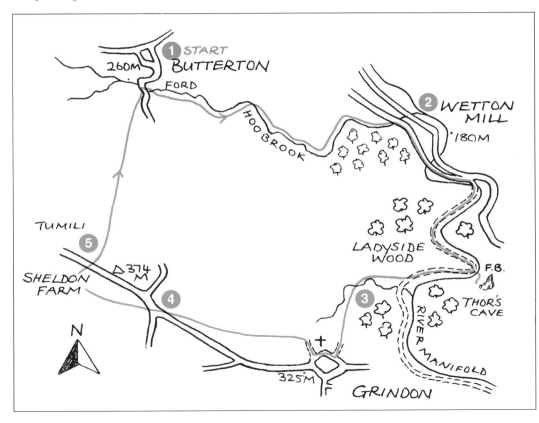

FACT FILE

Map OS Outdoor Leisure 24: The White Peak
Start/Finish SK 075563: Butterton, which can be reached by bus
Length 5½ miles (9km)
Walking time 3½ hours, longer if excursion to Thor's Cave is taken
Difficulty A fair amount of height change, including a couple of stiff ascents

The Route in Brief

1 SK 075563. Cross Hoo Brook at bottom of village and follow it SE, then NE, down to Wetton Mill.
2 R following river to footbridge under Thor's Cave. Visit cave, return to river, then W up and out of Ladyside Wood. Keep to R of brook.
3 Cross brook and climb to Grindon. R to church and take L of 2 stiles. Head W turning WNW over fields to road at Grindonmoor Gate.
4 Cross road to opposite stile, cross paddock and then fields WNW to Sheldon Farm, turning hard R just before it almost 180° NE to stile on to road. Cross road.
5 Cross tumuli to gate, then to stile at footpath sign. NE and NNE back to Butterton.

ALSTONEFIELD, MILLDALE AND WETTON

This walk, keeping just to the Staffordshire side of the border with Derbyshire, explores a famous stretch of the River Dove between Milldale and Dovedale along the west bank, avoiding the worst of the crowds, and also takes in two of the most attractive villages in the south Peak. It demonstrates the truth of the old saying: 'The best bits of Derbyshire are in Staffordshire.'

More than one ancient packhorse route, delightful to tread, leads to Alstonefield, where markets were held in the late Middle Ages and where the George pub proves beyond doubt that it *is* possible to cater for locals and tourists alike, doing both superbly well. There is also a tea-room and a shop.

From the centre of the village **(1)** pass Alstonefield Hall, built in 1587 by John Harpur, and then St Peter's church which is worth entering. It has seventeenth-century box pews and a two-decker pulpit, next door to which is the canopied pew used by Charles Cotton, the writer, fisherman and friend of Izaak Walton,

who lived not far away at Beresford Hall (see Walk 31).

Take the first footpath to the right and descend steeply to Milldale, turning right to the bridge, passing a small shop. This is Viator's Bridge, an ancient packhorse bridge so called because Viator, the traveller, dismounts to cross it in *The Compleat Angler*, fearing it to be too narrow for his horse.

Turn right up the path just before the bridge, climbing steeply, and follow the river south along its west bank. Walk up through a wood and out on to pastureland before descending to the boggy riverside again. The river bends round to the right, opposite the Dove Holes (two caves) on the other bank, and then to the left. Before a stoutly built stone wall the path turns right up Hall Dale **(2)**, with Hurt's Wood on the left. These two names refer to Casterne Hall and the Hurt family, whose land's northern boundary is nearby. Hurt's Wood is considered to be one of the finest semi-natural ash woods in the country.

The path climbs relentlessly northwest up Hall Dale to Stanshope, a hamlet of a couple of

Milldale

farms and fine Stanshope Hall, partly and unusually of red brick, which offers accommodation and excellent dinners. Turn right at the road and left at the footpath after Grange Farm. Cross a series of stiles northwest over the fields and a lane. Turn left at the road, then immediately right over a stile. Turn left over a stile a few yards up the wall and walk into Wetton **(3)**.

Apart from a few caravans on its outskirts, the ancient settlement of Wetton has changed little over the centuries. It has one or two particularly fine farm buildings and, in the Royal Oak, a good pub that welcomes walkers. Take the lane signed 'Hartington and Hulme End' and after Town End Farm cross a stile on the right in the corner of the field by the lane leading off to the right. Alstonefield is now in sight over the fields to the east. Head in that direction, descending the first field diagonally to a stile in the corner. Note Wetton Hill (1,175ft/358m), a landmark for many miles around, to the northwest, and the tree-fringed hummock of Steep Low ahead to the northeast.

Turn right into an old green lane **(4)** and descend muddily. Turn right at the lane past Brook Lodge and shortly left at the footpath sign. Walk down the fields past a farm to the bottom of the dale, Steep Low now to the north. Climb to the left of two stiles along a bank, cross a lane and ascend the pastures back to Alstonefield.

Opposite: Wetton Hill

Map OS Outdoor Leisure 24: The White Peak
Start/Finish SK 131556: Alstonefield, which can be reached by bus
Length 5¾ miles (9km)
Walking time 3 hours
Difficulty A steep descent and one uphill slog

The Route in Brief

1 SK 131556. 1st footpath to R past church down to Milldale. R up path before bridge. Follow river S till after big bends to R and L.
2 R at stone wall up Hall Dale to Stanshope. R at road and L at path after Grange Farm. Cross stiles and road NW into Wetton.
3 Take lane signed 'Hartington'. R over stile after Town End Farm and E.
4 R into green lane, R at road and L at path. Past farm to dale bottom, up to L of 2 stiles in bank and back to start.

119

TISSINGTON

Beginning and ending along a disused railway line, this route begins at the charming village of Tissington, visits its neighbour, Parwich, and rises and falls over some lovely, unspoilt farmland and pasture, eventually passing an ancient manor house.

Tissington is a main contender for 'prettiest village in the Peak' award, and therefore suffers from a surfeit of tourists, particularly when the six wells are dressed for Ascension Day each year. This ceremony celebrates the purity and abundance of the water, which is said to have prevented the Black Death from striking down the community in the fourteenth century, and to have kept flowing throughout the severe drought of 1615.

The village has been almost completely unchanged for many years and is owned by the ancient family of FitzHerbert, who have lived here since the Middle Ages. Their beautiful hall dates from the early 1600s. The delightful church of St Mary is Norman in origin and has many interesting features.

The walk begins at the car park on the Tissington Trail **(1)**, which follows the line of the old Ashbourne to Buxton railway (closed 1967). Head north up it for over half a mile (1km). Shortly before the bridge, turn left up some wooden steps, cross the bridge, and take the track leading towards Shaw's Farm, shortly turning right at the footpath sign. The views over the valley ahead are thoroughly inviting. Walk northeast towards them, heading downhill past handsome Shaw's Farm, across the brook and up the other side, larks singing above. The village of Parwich now comes into sight. Walk downhill into it, emerging on to the green **(2)**.

Parwich is a thriving village of some 500 inhabitants, and can still boast church, chapel, school, post office, shop, cricket field, care centre and pub (the friendly Sycamore Inn). The fine hall was put up in the 1740s by the Levinge family, on the site of an older house. Unusually for the area, it is built of red brick.

Turn right on to the road and walk southeast out of the village, turning right at a footpath sign to Lea Hall at the end of the playing field. Follow the track to the pumping station, and turn right at the track and then at the gate. A

Near the start, the ancient burial ground at Minninglow on the horizon

very boggy and overgrown track now leads to open fields which in turn bring you to Sitterlow Farm **(3)**. Go through the farmyard and straight across the field ahead. Once through the gate, turn left almost immediately through another. Cross this field diagonally to the opposite corner and take the footbridge over Bletch Brook. Cross the large field ahead to the stile. Gorsehill Farm is on your left, with the Norman tower of All Saints' church at Bradbourne further east up the hill. Turn

round to survey the view back to Parwich, with the old hospital prominent above it.

Follow the hedge on the left, where foxgloves grow in profusion in the summer. When it turns to the left by a gate, continue straight ahead to a tree and an old stone gatepost, and straight on down to find a stile to the left of two ash trees. This part of the walk can be confusing, as the footpath disappears. If in doubt, head due south. Either way, climb the bank ahead and continue south

to the small road leading to Tissington **(4)**. Spare a glance for lovely Bradbourne Mill to the east in the valley bottom.

At the road, take the farm lane opposite leading south to Lea Cottage Farm. Walk through the farmyard, bearing right up the track rather than descending to Lea Hall. This ancient place passed through the hands of several old families, including the Bradbournes, before eventually being acquired by the FitzHerberts. When the track begins to peter out, head for the stile by the gate at the end of the wall on the right and cross the pasture to the gate in the far right corner by the brook in the trees. Cross and pass through a small gate on the right shortly afterwards and strike uphill diagonally towards the trees, passing between two posts, then swing right towards a gap in the trees by another brook.

Cross it and head up half-left to a gate in the hedge and on south, up across the next field to Woodeaves Farm **(5)**. Walk through the farmyard, keeping to the left of the bulk of the buildings but to the right of the new barn, and out along the track leading southwest.

A few steps after the big bend take a stile in the fence on the right and walk slightly left to a stile by a gate. Now walk downhill (southwest) past Lees Farm, crossing the farm road, and across meadows and stiles, southwest, west and southwest, to Fenny Bentley.

Fenny Bentley Old Hall

Fenny Bentley Old Hall, which lies to the south just before the road and is now known as Cherry Orchard Farm, incorporates a square tower which is all that is left of a large castellated mansion, then moated, which dates back to the fourteenth century or earlier. It was the long-time home of the Beresford family, and the church contains an alabaster monument to Thomas Beresford, his wife Agnes and their sixteen sons and five daughters. Every Beresford in the world is said to descend from them, and they hold an annual convention in the village, but whether or not they resemble their forebears they are unable to tell, as the sculptor enveloped all his figures in shrouds. Thomas Beresford, eight of his sons and their retainers formed a troop of horse under Henry V and fought with distinction at Agincourt.

Cross the road **(6)** (the Coach and Horses pub lies down the hill) and take the path opposite past the church. Turn right after the school and cross Ashes Lane to the footpath signposted 'Thorpe', leading west. As you crest the brow of the hill, the unmistakable shapes of Hamston and Thorpe Cloud hills come into view ahead. They are the first hills of the Peak District and thus the Pennine Range which leads to Scotland. Cross the Wash Brook in the next little valley, climb up to the Tissington Trail and turn right for the tramp north-northwest back to Tissington, the banks lined with a mass of wild flowers in the spring and summer.

FACT FILE

Map OS Outdoor Leisure 24: The White Peak
Start/Finish SK 178521: car park at Tissington, which can be reached by bus
Length 8 miles (13km)
Walking time 4½ hours
Difficulty Easy enough walking, but a compass might come in handy where the paths are indistinct and badly signed

The Route in Brief

1 SK 178521. N up Tissington Trail for ½ mile (1km). Cross bridge and take track then fields NE and NNE to Parwich.
2 R on to road by green, R at end of playing field towards 'Lea Hall' and S along track then fields to Sitterlow Farm.
3 Through yard, S across fields to footbridge over brook, and S uphill, briefly down with Gorsehill Farm to E, and uphill again to road to Tissington.
4 Cross road S to Lea Cottage Farm, bear SSW to brook in wood, SW to next brook, then S to Woodeaves Farm.
5 Out of farmyard on track SW and take stile in fence on R after bend, jinking briefly N before descending SW to Fenny Bentley.

6 Cross road, take path past church and school, then R across lane and W to Tissington Trail, turning R (NNW) back to Tissington.

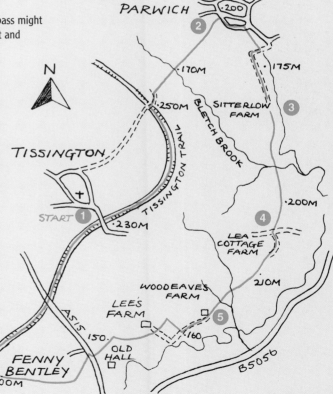

123

DANEBRIDGE AND WINCLE MINN

The lush wooded valleys of the Dane River and its western tributary the Shell Brook lie in pleasing contrast to the starker and bleaker high ground around them. This most westerly of our walks revels in the contrast, providing easy riverbank strolling, some more strenuous striding through pastures, and a couple of tough ascents.

This walk is entirely in Cheshire, but only just – the Dane River here forming the border with Staffordshire before wriggling and curling its way across the Cheshire plain. From the bridge **(1)** we turn left into the drive of Danebridge Fisheries and right at the stile along the fence and up to the tall, terraced cottages. Turn left at the road and take the stile in the wall on the left past the Ship Inn (free house). Bonnie Prince Charlie is said to have stopped here on his march south to claim his throne, carelessly leaving behind his gun and a few other possessions. Well, his spree would soon be over.

The Conduit at Hammond's Hole

Cross the field to the next stile, then a lane, and continue along the wall and up steeply through the wood. Cross the next field half-right and turn left on to the lane. Pass a pond on the left and go through a gate leading down a track past Wincle Grange **(2)**. This ancient building was a Cistercian priory in the Middle Ages and is said to have an underground passage to Wincle church.

Pick up the footpath descending westerly over stiles. Congleton Edge can be seen proudly standing out to the southwest. Turn right and quickly left over stiles near a farm to drop by a terraced track into a large pasture. Aim west to the wood at the valley bottom, heading for a curve in the trees indicating a bend in the Shell Brook. Do not cross the footbridge; instead turn right and walk northeast along the brook a short way to a stile on the left. Cross it and ford the brook **(3)**, continuing straight ahead with the brook on the left. The path becomes broader as it climbs through the wood. Reach a wide brackeny clearing and keep on until the path splits at a solitary hawthorn. Fork right and continue, soon descending generally northerly, crossing a tiny brook, then a stile, then fording a larger brook and ascending the other side of the valley, the brook on the left.

Climb out of the wood, Lower Greasley Farm becoming visible ahead. The going may be muddy as you reach a farm track. Turn right for a few paces and then go left over a stile past the gate. Skirt the farm buildings **(4)** and find a stile in the fence at the edge of the wood at Greasley Hollow. Descend to ford the brook at the stile and climb steeply, scrambling up the bank as best you can to a stile at the top. Now walk up the broad grassy spine of Nabbs Hill, curving round to the right at the top to a stile. Fine views have opened up behind to the south.

Cross the stile and continue through the gate, turning left up the track at Butterlands Farm. The Ordnance Survey map is confusing here. Follow the track as it swings round to the left and leads south-southwest. Higher Greasley Farm is now visible ahead. Keep on towards it as the track ducks away to the southeast. Reach the farm **(5)**, and at the gate above the farmhouse zig-zag up the path to reach the road at the top of the ridge, known as Wincle Minn. You have now attained 1,230ft (375m) and can relax, because it is mainly downhill home. Turn left and walk south, feasting your eyes on the views. To the west is Cheshire laid out below, with Jodrell Bank easily discernible. To the southwest is the

125

Map OS Outdoor Leisure 24: The White Peak
Start/Finish SK 965652: Danebridge, Wincle.
Wincle can be reached by bus from Leek, Longnor and elsewhere
Length 7³/₄ miles (12.5km)
Walking time 4 hours

Difficulty Two or three strenuous climbs. The fording of several brooks requires waterproof boots, and a compass would be useful

The Route in Brief

1 SK 965652. L into Fisheries drive, R at stile up to cottages, L past pub, cross fields to stile, cross lane, climb through wood, ¹/₂R over field, L at lane and take track after pond past Grange.
2 Path leads W. R and L near farm, W down to wood, R along brook and over stile to ford brook.
3 Climb through wood, forking R when path splits. Down across brook, stile, and larger brook, up through wood, R at track and L at stile past farm.
4 Stile in fence leads across brook. Scramble up bank to stile, ascend grassy spine to farm, L up track and straight on towards farm when track ducks SE.
5 Zig-zag up to road, L round bend, L at farm and follow Gritstone Trail signs across brook.
6 Up woods and follow signs SW across River Dane and E and NE along it, crossing halfway, back to start.

Cloud, guarding the northern approach to Congleton Edge. Behind to the northeast is Shutlingsloe Hill (see Walk 23), and to the north the radio mast near Sutton Common. Follow the road as it bears left and turn left at Hawksloe Farm, passing to the right of the buildings.

Descend steadily southeast and east down the pasture and then through the woods, following Gritstone Trail signs. There are more views, this time of Hen Cloud and the Roaches to the east-southeast (see Walk 26). Cross the Shell Brook again (6) and climb easterly through the woods. Go right as signed by the hedge at the top of a field rather than climbing the stile by the gate. Pass a small ruined barn and descend. We are now heading south-southwest with further glorious views. Follow the signs down over the beautiful airy pastures, Cartlidge Wood to the right, to cross the River Dane at the footbridge

Walk up the lane and then along the river east and northeast till crossing to the north bank at a footbridge by a weir and continuing, eventually passing Pringle Cottage and walking up the drive of the Fisheries back to the bridge.

GOLDEN HILL AND THE HAMPS

Set deep in the western moorlands, this is a lonely and richly enjoyable walk through one of the Peak's less-fashionable areas, following the line of the River Hamps. Golden Hill has a simple and unsung beauty and a strenuous climb up the Elkstone Slope provides wonderful views of Staffordshire's finest country.

Take the path on the right of the church (1) through the farmyard, leading west up a track with sycamore, beech and rowan bordering a deep brook on the right. Just before the gate cross the brook and turn right up the line of trees to a stile and right again, heading northeast down a track with a good view of Onecote (pronounced 'Oncot') Grange and leading through a farmyard to a lane. Cross and continue down a very overgrown short stretch of path and across footbridges over brook and stream, turning right after the second over two cattle grids, through a gate, east, and on in front of the Grange and over the footbridge across the Hamps (2).

Now head east up the pasture towards the largest ash, passing through a stile in the wall beyond. Keep on east through a gap in the fence between ashes and on until you see a stile in the wall on the left. Head for that, turning northeast.

Walk through the farmyard, carrying on up the brook after the farmhouse and heading north up the pasture. At the summit there is a small barn. This is Golden Hill (3), which rises to 1,152ft (350m). It is well named, particularly when the morning and evening sun slants through the tips of the long pasture grasses, and its solitary beauty may be accompanied by the singing of larks overhead. There is a remote timelessness here that should be savoured.

In the field after the barn descend to cross the brook where hedges meet. Now head northeast diagonally across the field, crossing boggy ground, to a stile in a far corner. This is mushroom country. Keep north again, straight on, Brund Hays Farm ahead, and pick up the track leading down to Black Brook Farm (4). Tucked away from the eyes of the world, it strikes one as the perfect little farmstead, though it might have its drawbacks in the depths of winter.

Go through the yard and on over the brook, passing through a field of thorns. Now follow the brook north all the way up, turning right

The River Hamps at Onecote Grange

and immediately left at the lane past Breech Farm. A 425m (1,394ft) trig point appears on top of the modestly named Elkstone Slope to the west. (The hills around may try and deceive you into thinking they are higher, but they are lying.) Pass Under the Hill House and turn left just after, climbing very steeply to the summit (5), passing Hill House on the right. From here there are superb moorland views, particularly southeast back to the glorious

woods, dales and hills of the Manifold valley, punctuated by the twin spires of Butterton and Grindon, with that great landmark and powerful site, Hazelton Clump, on the distant skyline above Ilam. Below lies the wooded valley of the Warslow Brook, hurrying along from near the Mermaid Inn to join the Manifold at Ecton Bridge.

Continue west from the summit, over the road and down to the River Hamps, which is dammed at first to form a large pond. Turn left and walk south along it. Descend diagonally southwest after the dam to a footbridge and cross. Climb the bank and at the end of the trees turn left through a gate (not signed) and head southward along a path over the fields to the disused Mixon Copper Mine (6). There is a sense of quiet here, relief even, now that the noise, shouting, toil and bustle has slipped away in time.

Go past a charming farm, in the middle of nowhere at the end of two long tracks, and follow the track all the way back south to Onecote Grange, noticing the serpentine contortions the Hamps puts itself through. At the Grange fork left through the farm buildings, go right over the cattle grid, left at the road over the stream, and left at the road back to the church. The Jervis Arms alone fulfils the function that once it took at least five inns hereabouts to do.

Golden Hill, Onecote

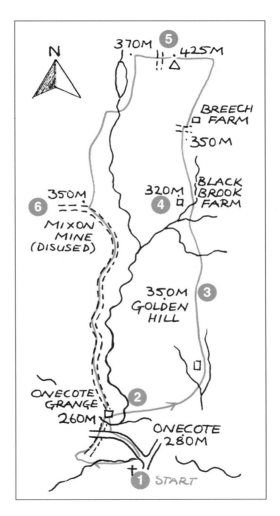

FACT FILE

Map OS Outdoor Leisure 24: The White Peak
Start/Finish SK 048552: Onecote church. There are buses to Onecote
Length 6¼ miles (10km)
Walking time 4 hours
Difficulty One very steep climb. A compass would be helpful

The Route in Brief

1 SK 048552. Path on R of church. Cross footbridge before gate, R up trees to stile, R again and NE to cross lane then footbridges. Pass in front of Grange and cross Hamps.
2 E to largest ash ahead, through stile in wall, through gap in fence between ashes, and L through stile in wall. NE through farm, over brook and N to Golden Hill.
3 Cross brook where hedges meet in field after barn and go diagonally across field NE to stile in far corner. N to Black Brook Farm.
4 Through yard, over brook and N, eventually crossing lane and on till L past Under the Hill House, climbing W to summit.
5 Descend W over road to river. L (S) to footbridge below dam. Cross, climb bank, L through gate after trees and S over fields to Mixon Mine.
6 Pass farm and S along track to Onecote Grange. L through farm buildings, R over grid, L at road over stream, and L at road back to church.

BRASSINGTON AND CARSINGTON

This is a fine airy walk for striding out across meadows and along tracks, much of it 'on the tops', with a great deal of interest on the way. It visits some rocks which are the haunt of climbers and a fascinating cave. There is one steep climb.

Brassington stands on the side of a hill (the name means 'farm by the steep path'). It has been a settlement for many centuries, and there have been various remains of early man found in the vicinity. The earliest turnpike into the Peak from the south was built to Brassington from Derby in the early eighteenth century. From Brassington, travellers took the limestone lanes to destinations further north, escaping the worst of the mud perhaps, but facing some severe conditions in winter. There were then several pubs in the village to look after them, of which two, the Miner's Arms and Ye Olde Gate, remain. Both welcome walkers, and the Gate is one of the most beautiful and well-run pubs in

Looking over Brassington towards the start

Derbyshire. Brassington was for long a major lead-mining centre, but now the various local quarries provide employment.

From the church (1), which dates from Norman times, walk downhill past the Miner's Arms, with splendid twin-gabled Tudor House ahead. Turn left and take the footpath immediately on the right, leaving the garden by the gate in the corner. Cross two fields before turning left in the third and following the wall up through the stile and then turning right.

Brassington is now stretched out behind and below. The way leads to Carsington largely east-southeast through fields, past old mines (2) and outcrops of limestone. Join a track, cross another and continue across a small and then a large field, slanting left at an old gatepost to the left of the rock formations. Where, shortly, the path divides, keep right, pointing towards the top of the far hill. Carsington Reservoir lies to the south.

The path becomes a wide track which skirts the hill and leads into Carsington village (3), where the Miner's Arms pub will provide refreshment. Carsington is another old lead-mining community and several of the cottages have mine shafts beneath them. Hopton Hall was for many centuries the home of the Gell

family until sold in 1989. They dubiously claimed descent from Gellius, a Roman centurion, after an urn was found nearby. Sir John Gell, the Parliamentary General, was born here. Another, less fortunate, local person is recorded in the church register. An entry for 29 September 1668 reads: 'Sarah Tissington died. Born without hands or arms. She learned to knit, dig in the garden and do other things with her feet.'

Turn left at the road up a small lane which leads between pretty cottages, climb some steps and pass through a swing gate into Carsington Pasture, 365 acres (148 ha) of open grazing land which rises to 1,073ft (327m). Follow the fence along and then climb the steep and often slippery path up the edge of the wood. Take care: there are many mine shafts in this area, not all of them capped. Turn left at the wall and walk up past the Lady Chair (marked on the Ordnance Survey map as the King's Chair). It would be interesting to know what Lady or King thinks about the recent intrusion of the reservoir into their age-old view. Personally, I admit to a bias against car parks, yacht clubs and public toilets where once there was a beautiful green valley, and the view is one I could do without. Note the fine, half-ruined Eniscloud Barn a

few fields away to the northeast, and, to the right just before the road, the remains of a windmill.

Cross the road and climb two stiles on to the High Peak Railway (1830–1967 and one of the earliest in the world), and turn right. Cross the road leading to the quarry and take the left-hand footpath leading north, signposted 'Grange Mill'. There are more mines to the right.

As the track bends to the left, continue straight on, keeping to the right of the wall. Turn left (northwest) along the gated track and then left over the cattle grid and follow the wall along to New Harboro' farm **(4)**, forlorn and desolate in its abandonment. Cross the stile and skirt to the right of the buildings. Go straight ahead through the gateway and, keeping southwest, climb the field ahead, aiming to the right of the solitary tree to a stile in the second of two parallel walls. Follow the line of the broken wall across Harboro' Rocks, the reservoir again coming into view. Continue towards the top, which reaches some 1,250ft (380m), providing wonderful views, and where there is both a trig point and a Neolithic tomb of about 2500 BC. Then strike leftwards (south), aiming towards the left of the quarry buildings. The tomb is only one of many exciting relics of early man which lie near or

Carsington Reservoir

along the line of the Portway, a prehistoric track which led from Wirksworth, via Alport to the Wye at Ashford. Do not miss the cave below. This was inhabited from at least the Bronze Age, and Daniel Defoe, in his *Tour Through Great Britain*, relates finding a family of six living in it. Some distance away to the northwest is Minninglow, crowned with a few unconvincing beech trees and the site of a Neolithic chambered tomb.

Find a stile leading on to the High Peak Trail (5) and cross it towards Brassington. Turn right at the road and, after 400 yards/metres, left, again signposted 'Brassington'. Follow the wall then fence down to a lane. Turn right here back into the village.

FACT FILE

Map OS Outdoor Leisure 24: The White Peak
Start/Finish SK 233544: Brassington, which can be reached by bus
Length 5 miles (8km)
Walking time 3 hours
Difficulty Easy enough but for one very steep climb

The Route in Brief

1 SK 233544. Downhill from church, L then immediately R at footpath across fields, past mineworkings on L.
2 Continue ESE to Carsington.
3 L at junction and up through cottages to Carsington Pasture. Follow line of wood, then wall N. Cross road, R on to High Peak Trail, and L (N) towards Grange Mill. Keep straight N when track bends L, turn L at next track and L at cattle grid to farm.
4 Skirt farm and climb SW to Harboro' Rocks, then S to L of quarry.
5 Find stile to High Peak Trail and cross it, following signs back to Brassington.

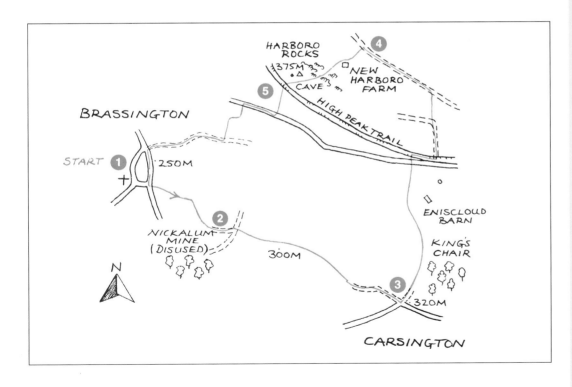

ALDERWASLEY

This most southeasterly of our walks is mainly across rolling farm and pasture land and offers the opportunity for some fairly easy striding out without any serious ascents or descents. It returns through Shining Cliff Woods, one of the most extensive and finest examples of old deciduous woodland in Derbyshire.

There is an ancient tradition of a battle here, but so long ago that it is obscured by the mists of time. Only field and farm names – Killcroft and Bury Hill – keep it alive today. St Margaret's Chapel dates from Henry VIII's reign but incorporates earlier features from an older building on the same site. It was for centuries the private chapel of the Hurt family and is reputedly haunted.

Walk down Chapel Hill **(1)**. Crich Stand, which will overlook much of the route, can be seen to the northeast. At 950ft (290m), it offers quite remarkable views across the Midlands. Ahead lie Shining Cliff Woods. Turn left into New Road at the junction and left down the footpath opposite the track to Home Farm, signed as the Midshires Way. Descend northerly over the meadows to a brook, then climb and fall again to Lane End and cross Mere Brook by the gates of Watergate Farm, forking uphill to the right by the pond.

Pass through a stile by a gate to meet a track, turning left. Pass two cottages and now deviate from the Midshires Way, forking left **(2)** at a footpath sign along a track round the edge of Bunting Wood on the left, and then Mill Wood on the right. Turn left just after the first house on the left and head south through the garden of Wigwell Mill, keeping to the left, through a gate and across Mere Brook again. Ascend the edge of the wood, forking right where it juts out to cross a stile over a track and heading up the field ahead almost due south to the corner of Long Wood. Walk round the gorsey tip of the plantation, and turn east at a sign to Alderwasley, then south through a gate and along the track to Knob Farm **(3)**.

Continue down to the junction of lanes and go straight over, down the drive then path

leading past Bury Hill Farm. Halfway along the garden wall fork right through a stile and continue down to a gate. Cross Pendleton Brook and walk south up the wall to the next gate. Cross the field south to where the left-hand wall meets the buildings of Little Hayes Farm, turning right at a stile in front of Allsop's Cottage and continuing up the path along the wall northwest to the lane by Willett's Farm **(4)**. Turn right, then shortly left (southwest), signed 'Alport Heights'. Continue past a lane where the hedge ends, and up the wall. Fork left (southeast), cutting off the top corner of the next field but one and making for the three-gabled Ye Olde Bear Inn.

Cross the road to the path leading south opposite. Cross a brook and continue over the fields, turning left at the track leading past Sandhall Farm. Cross the road at the junction and take the path ahead leading south. In the second, large, field, head southwest to a stile in the wall near a single hawthorn. Then walk up left of the wall, south-southwest, to a lane **(5)**.

Cross and continue over the meadows, aiming south-southwest for a gate in the far corner of the third large one, and to the end of the wall ahead in the fifth. Keep on up the wall which forms a right angle, southwest veering south, keeping Scots pines, gorse and bracken to the left.

Continue southeast over a lane, past the edge of a wood, and down a muddy track. Pass a stile on the left by some hawthorns and a hollybush and take the next stile on the left just

through the next gateway. Now head northeast to find a Midshires Way sign 75 yards/metres left of some ash trees **(6)** and continue in the same direction towards the distant Crich Stand, the sun perhaps flashing off the sheer white cliff below it.

Follow the Midshires Way signs, crossing a marshy brook and turning right at Palerow Lane. Pass a lane coming in from the left, turn right at Belper Road and shortly left at the Midshires Way sign. Follow the path northeast to Netherpark Farm. Turn right at the lane, pass the plantation on the right and turn left down the path by the bungalow opposite Wiggonlea Farm **(7)**.

Walk into Beggars Well Wood. Round the bend by the well and, after a while, take the

Above: Shining Cliff Woods
Opposite: The track between Bunting and Mill Woods

broad path coming in from the left, almost doubling back on yourself and heading west. Continue to the pool where a pipe seemingly throws the water uphill and turn hard right, following the Youth Hostel arrows and heading northeast. Turn left (north), following the red and white arrows, and then take the path which runs up past the Youth Hostel at Shining Cliff and on westward through Typeclose Plantation **(8)**.

The path passes a brackeny clearing to the right and then swings northwest. Another path comes in from the left; keep on round the

Map OS Outdoor Leisure 24: The White Peak
Start/Finish SK 324534: St Margaret's Chapel, Alderwasley. There are buses and trains to Ambergate, from where it is possible to walk up to Beggars Well Wood and join the route
Length 8½ miles (13.5km)
Walking time 5 hours
Difficulty Easy walking. A compass would be useful

The Route in Brief

1 SK 324534. Down Chapel Hill, L at junction, L at path, following Midshires Way signs till passing a pond and then 2 cottages.

2 L at footpath sign along track past woods. L after house on L and S past Long Wood to Knob Farm.

3 Straight over junction of lanes past Bury Hill Farm, forking R (S) over brook to Little Hayes Farm, then NW along wall to lane by Willett's Farm.

4 R, then L towards Alport Heights. Keep SW, then SE to Ye Olde Bear Inn. Cross road and go S across brook till L at track past Sandhall Farm. Cross road to path ahead and SSW to lane.

5 SW veering S to cross next lane, down track to 2nd stile on L, then NE to Midshires Way sign.

6 Follow Midshires Way signs to Netherpark Farm. R at road and L opposite Wiggonlea Farm.

7 Take broad path in woods coming in from L and hard R at pool. To and past Youth Hostel and on W.

8 Path swings NW after clearing. Exit wood NNE and leave next wood NW towards Hall. R at lane and L back to chapel.

sharp right bend where another path joins from the left. Leave the wood, following the path along the wall north-northeast, and enter Park Plantation, a birch wood. Leave northwest towards Alderwasley Hall (pronounced 'Arraslee'), a plain Georgian building with an Elizabethan core, which reluctantly reveals part of itself through the trees. Home of the Hurt family and their forebears since the thirteenth century, it is now a school, and the well-maintained park once again has a herd of deer. It only remains to pass the war memorial and turn right up the lane and left at the junction back to the old chapel.

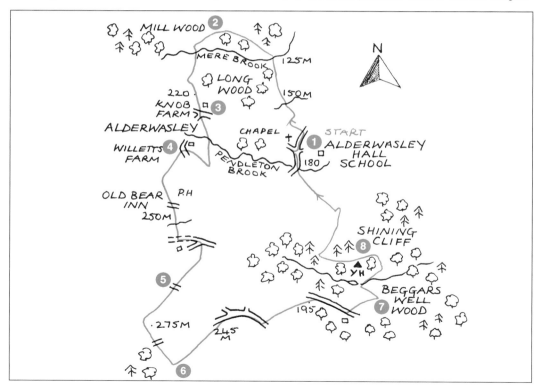

THE CALDON CANAL AND COMBES VALLEY

This varied walk begins with a leisurely stroll along the Caldon Canal and River Churnet then climbs and dips over pasture and farm land, returning to Cheddleton via the wooded valley of the Combes Brook. It offers a thoroughly satisfying and enjoyable ramble through some of the prettiest North Staffordshire scenery.

The walk begins at the Boat pub on the east tip of Cheddleton village (1). Park here if you intend to refresh yourself before or after your walk. There is otherwise limited space on the lane near the old station across the canal, river and railway line. From the Boat, cross Basford Bridge and turn right (south) along the towpath of the Caldon Canal, the lovely River Churnet flowing parallel to the east. In the summer months great willowherb, meadowsweet and arrowhead are among the wild flowers which grow in profusion on the banks.

The canal was begun in 1779, engineered by James Brindley, a Derbyshire man. It originally ran from Etruria, the site of the Wedgwood pottery factory in Hanley, to Froghall, over 17 miles (28km) east. The North Staffordshire Railway built the line alongside the canal in 1849 and eventually bought the canal. Both fell into disuse after the last war. The canal was reclaimed from dereliction and reopened to navigation in 1974.

Walk south along the towpath. It is an intensely peaceful scene and your reverie is unlikely to be disturbed by anything more intrusive than the quacking of a duck, the scuttling of a water vole, the skitting of a moorhen or coot, or the slow passing burble of one of several narrowboats that ply this stretch of water. Ahead, on the other side, the mixed conifers of Consall Wood dominate the view. After a mile (1.5km) pass a restored wooden drawbridge and then after another 500 yards/metres reach Oakmeadow Ford Lock. The canal drops to the level of the river here and their paths merge. Cross over the bridge to the other side and continue, alders lining the opposite bank. After another half-mile (1km) you will find a couple of mileposts. Partially obscured by trees behind them are two disused lime kilns. After another half-mile you will reach Consall Forge.

The Caldon Canal

137

This powerful place should be savoured. It was once the site of a busy water-powered iron works, and it is not difficult to imagine the bangings and clangings, shouts and bustle of those not-so-far-off days. Some 2,000 men are thought to have worked here in its heyday. Now the scene is one of peace and reflection. Semi-natural woodland surrounds the spot. A couple of narrowboats are likely to be moored up, and one or two pipe-smoking types may be tinkering about with those little jobs that only boat-owners can find to keep themselves occupied. The river parts from the canal here, and the railway line runs between the river

The North Staffordshire Steam Railway at Cheddleton

bank and the Black Lion pub.

Cross to the pub (2) and take the path between it and the small barn to the left up the steps through Crowgutter Wood. This is known as the Devil's Staircase. Now follow the lovely path towards Belmont Hall, one of several houses hereabouts associated for a long time with the Sneyd family. Turn right down the lane for a few steps (3), then right again, down a path through the wood, right at the next lane and up round a bend. Now turn left at the footpath sign. Cross the fields northeast and climb to a stile the other side of red-roofed Hey House. Now follow the clearly signed path running easterly past ancient Odda Hall and past a trig point which at 896ft (273m) is some 450ft (137m) higher than Consall Forge, to meet a track leading to Stocks Green past the church of St Leonard, the patron saint of prisoners.

Turn left at the junction (4) and then fork left, turning half-right into the grounds of the last house on the right to a stile in the wall ahead. Now cross the fields northerly to the left of the white house ahead, forking right at the track. Go through the gateway of the house at the end and turn left over the stile halfway down the little drive.

The path now leads northwest (5), keeping to the left-hand side of the fields down to a woodside track across a little ford. It is usually boggy here, and there is an ancient feeling to this beautiful old lane. Cross a track and continue along a path past Whitehough, with

its many blocked-up windows. The house dates from 1620 and was built for the Whitehall family. Keep to the left-hand wall of the big field beyond. Cross the stile and head right to the stile by the gate in the wall to the right of the little barn.

The Ordnance Survey map now suggests the path carries on through the middle of the impenetrable thicket ahead. Instead walk right-handed round the edge of the thicket and, as it ends, head half-left to find a stile near the corner of the field. Now follow the track down for a few paces (6) before turning right over a stile and along the path leading through the rhododendrons of Whitehough Wood. Turn left down the track at the end of the wood, then right at the gate through the RSPB nature reserve at the top of Low Wood, forking left down the path as the track slopes upwards. Sharpcliffe Hall is just to the northeast. This substantial house was begun in 1679, another residence of the Whitehall family. Fork left again as the path splits into two, cross the Combes Brook and climb out of the wood.

Now head northwest up the broad fields ahead (7), sometimes ploughed and sown, to Upper Ferneyhill Farm, keeping to the right of the buildings to the stiles in fences and wall and down the field to the road. Turn left, then right after Lowerhouse Farm down the track, heading west, Cheddleton now in view. Pass the ancient Buttercross at the crossing of paths and continue past the Steam Railway back to the start.

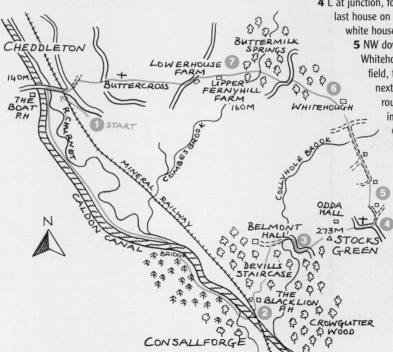

The Buttercross outside Cheddleton

Map OS Outdoor Leisure 24: The White Peak; OS Pathfinder 810: Ashbourne and the Churnet Valley
Start/Finish SK 982521: Cheddleton, near The Boat pub. Cheddleton can be reached by bus
Length 7½ miles (12km)
Walking time 4 hours
Difficulty Easy apart from one fairly steep climb

The Route in Brief

1 SK 982521. S down canal to Consall Forge.
2 Take Devil's Staircase up past Black Lion and follow path.
3 R down lane, R down path through wood, R up lane and L at footpath. Follow path NE and ENE past Hey House and Odda Hall to Stocks Green.
4 L at junction, fork L, ½R into grounds of last house on R and over stile. N to white house, R at track, L over stile.
5 NW down over brook and up to Whitehough. Along L edge of big field, then to R of little barn in next. Head NW in next, but rounding thicket on R, to stile in corner.
6 R over next stile through rhododendrons, L down track at wood's end, R at gate through nature reserve, L down path as track slopes up, L as path splits, across brook and up out of wood.
7 NW ahead up fields to farm, L then R at road down track, W, back to Cheddleton.

OUSAL DALE AND DIMMINGSDALE

This most southerly of the walks in this book is a gentle ramble through the well-watered woods and pastures that make up the swathe of lovely countryside south of the village of Oakamoor. It offers a remarkable contrast to the windswept rigours of the Dark Peak.

From the car-park (1) follow signs for the Woodland Walk, heading NW up the Staffordshire Way, and following the water until keeping right at Earls Rock House (ignore the footpath to the Old Forge). The derelict smelting mill was built in the 1740s and was soon converted to grind corn. There would once have been quite a little community living and working here.

Continue up through the peace and quiet of Ousal Dale, the track becoming sandy as it leads through the conifers and is joined by others from left and right. At the end of the wood turn left (south), off the Staffordshire Way past the Youth Hostel (2) and down through the Ranger nature reserve, a lovely retreat of wilderness and calm with many rare plants and birds. The turreted hulk of Alton Towers can be spotted to the east. This massive mansion, now semi-ruined, was built and then abandoned by the earls of Shrewsbury during the nineteenth century. It forms a Gothic silhouette to the famous amusement park, whose roller-coasters, shouts and cavortings seem a million miles away from this quiet spot.

Leave the clearing past a memorial to Paul Rey, rambler and traveller, and descend through the conifers to cross the river (3), a tributary of the Churnet. Notice the little round house upstream. Ignore tracks to left and right and take the uphill track straight ahead signposted 'Gentleman's Rock' and shortly 'Threap Wood', climbing in a generally westerly direction to reach a stile at the edge of the wood.

Slant left, following Staffordshire Moorlands Walk markers around the edge of the wood and heading southwesterly, over a stile, to the left of a pair of oak trees in the field ahead and on to a stile in the corner. Follow the wall for a few paces before turning left over stiles and two fields to a track.

Turn right here and head north, with fine views across the wooded landscape towards the

Left: The Round House in Dimmingsdale
Right: Autumn in Dimmingsdale

FACT FILE

Map OS Pathfinder 810: Ashbourne and the Churnet Valley

Start/Finish SK 063432: car park less than a mile (1.5km) northwest of Alton, which can be reached by bus, on the 'Red Road' to Oakamoor by Lord's Bridge

Length 4 miles (6.5km)

Walking time 2½ hours

Difficulty Easy tracks and paths with a couple of moderate climbs

The Route in Brief

1 SK 063432. Sign for Woodlands Walk leads NW up Staffordshire Way. Keep R at Earls Rock House and turn L at end of wood.

2 S past Youth Hostel, through the Ranger reserve to river.

3 Cross river and take uphill path ahead, W, to edge of wood. Head SW, following SMW markers to track. Turn R and head N to pond.

4 L at footpath and across pasture to wood, follow SMW signs through it to track and N across hilly pasture to gate near houses. R down lane and R down path towards Dimmingsdale.

5 Cross brook and head SE past pools. Cross stream where it bends L and up 2 sets of steps. Path leads E beside wood and past cottage; double back NW to start on path climbing parallel on L.

Hawksmoor Nature Reserve, while the pinnacles of Alton Towers again appear to the east. Turn left at the footpath sign above the pond **(4)** and cross the pasture to the stile at the wood, following the Staffordshire Moorlands Walk signs through it west-northwest, descending to a track. Turn left, then soon right at an SMW sign. Cross the hilly pasture in a northerly direction and keep well to the left of the wooden barn to pick up a track leading to a stile by a gate near some houses. Turn right down the lane and shortly right again down a path signed 'Dimmingsdale'.

Cross the brook **(5)** and continue alongside it, past a little waterfall and through Dimmingsdale Wood. Redstarts, kingfishers and wood warblers can regularly be seen here. Cross the stream again and continue southeast as it widens into pools and then lakes.

After the water narrows to a stream again, and as it bends round to the left, cross the footbridge, climb the steps to a track and then more steps. Emerge by a stile on to a brackeny bank and head east along the path beside Threap Wood, with an outcrop of rocks above. The top of an Alton Towers ride or two and then the turrets of the house can be glimpsed in the distance, accompanied by frenzied screams and yells. Continue past a cottage to join a gravelled track. After a while spy a raised path climbing almost parallel to your left. Double back on this, northwest to your starting point, where the Ramblers' Retreat café will produce delicious home-cooking.

INDEX

Page numbers in *italics* indicate illustrations

ACKNOWLEDGEMENTS

The author would like to thank Mike Williams for his superb photographs which speak more eloquently than many words, and for checking the route directions; and Susannah Penrose, for her maps, company and encouragement.

The publishers would like to thank Roland Smith of the Peak National Park for his comments on this book.

The following accompanied us on our walks: Jerry Penrose, Sarah Penrose, Peter Ariowitsch, Lotte Courts, Mike Williams, Simon Aylmer, Jane Charteris, Pete Clark, Andy Grainger, Charlie Penrose, Emma Penrose, Lallie Shepherd, Diane Tranter, Kate Tranter, Zusi Villiers, Bryan Williams.